The Tenth Muse
An Anthology

ANTHONY ASTBURY is a poet and anthologist, and the founder of the Greville Press.

MICHAEL SCHMIDT is the author of *Lives of the Poets* (1999) and the five-volume *Story of Poetry* (2001–).

Also from Carcanet

Thomas Blackburn
Selected Poems edited by Julia Blackburn

W.S. Graham
The Nightfisherman: Selected Letters
edited by Michael and Margaret Snow

Robert Graves
Complete Poems, 3 volumes
A Survey of Modernist Poetry (with Laura Riding)

Anne Ridler
Collected Poems

C.H. Sisson
Collected Poems
Collected Translations
Poems: Selected

Helen Thomas, with Myfanwy Thomas
Under Storm's Wing

David Wright
Poems and Versions
To the Gods the Shades

The Tenth Muse
An Anthology

Edited by Anthony Astbury
With a preface by Michael Schmidt

CARCANET

in association with
the Greville Press

For Antonia and Harold

First published in Great Britain in 2005 by
Carcanet Press Limited
Alliance House
Cross Street
Manchester M2 7AQ

Individual selections first published by The Greville Press, 6 Mellors Court,
The Butts, Warwick CV34 4ST
Preface © Michael Schmidt 2005

Acknowledgements of permission to reprint in-copyright material can be
found on pp. 259–61 and constitute an extension of the copyright page.

The publisher acknowledges financial assistance from Arts Council England

Typeset in Monotype Garamond by XL Publishing Services, Tiverton
Printed and bound in England by SRP Ltd, Exeter

CONTENTS

'Too Far to Hear the Singing': Poems by Lawrence Durrell,
selected by Françoise Kestsman Durrell

Poems by David Gascoyne, selected by Judy Gascoyne

Poems by W.S. Graham, selected by Nessie Dunsmuir

'Yesterday Only' and other poems: Poems by Robert Graves, selected by Beryl Graves

Poems by C.H. Sisson, selected by Nora Sisson

Poems by Elizabeth Smart, selected by Sebastian Barker

Poems by David Wright, selected by Oonagh Swift

PREFACE

Hesiod was the first poet whom the immortal muses constrained to sing. A mere rustic lad, shepherding his flock on the skirts of Mount Helicon, he was surprised by these nine elegant ladies, daughters of Zeus, who lectured him on lying and on truth-telling and then commanded him to sing. This he did, naming them, and spilling forth a cosmic poem about the gods and the order of all creation, a poem brimming with knowledge and wisdom he did not himself possess.[1] And from that date to this the poet who sings beyond him- or herself is thought to receive some inspiration, some grace, from an agency it still pleases us to call 'the muses' or 'a muse'. Hesiod met immortal muses; nowadays we content ourselves with mortal ones.

In 1911 Edward Thomas published *The Tenth Muse*, a book sufficiently popular to be reissued twice in the following decade. It considered the love poems of English poets from Chaucer to Shelley, in particular reflecting upon the human muses who elicited such verse from such men.[2] It seemed to me appropriate to entitle this anthology *The Tenth Muse* as a tribute to the late Myfanwy Thomas and by extension to all those individuals, male and female, who inspire, stand by, promote or memorialise the work of poets to whose lives they have been central. Anthony Astbury agreed.

Imagine what we might learn from Philippa Chaucer's or Mary (not to mention poor Harriet) Shelley's selection of their spouse's poems… learn about who they were, how they saw their partner's art, and how they reflected upon their own reflections, as it were, in that art. Anthony Astbury, poet, anthologist and founder of the Greville Press, set out a decade ago to provide us with such selections and reflections in the modern period. He invited poets' spouses and others close to them (sons, daughters, 'significant others') to make their selections of what they most valued in the writer's work. Each 'muse' made a selection and provided a note, and the resulting selections were published in handsome Greville Press chapbooks. This anthology brings those chap-

1 *The Theogony*
2 The book expanded upon Chapter VIII of *Feminine Influence on the Poets* (1910).

books together in an amazing composite anthology whose coherence is its wonderful diversity of affection and response.

The breadth of the book is century-wide, from Edward Thomas writing before and during the First World War to Harold Pinter writing today. There is something of a bias towards the poets who emerged from the creative disorders of the late 1930s and 1940s, a period when English poetry was in a struggle with politics, Modernisms and war. This is the generation just before Astbury's, the one by which he took his bearings. The legacy of that creative disorder (always the best order for art) still has much to teach. The muses who make these selections do not limit themselves to poetry of biographical interest. We come to understand, in the variety of work to which they positively respond, why they were such important readers and enablers: a muse inspires and a muse assesses what has been inspired. It is as though, on the skirts of Mount Helicon, the immortal muses had lingered to appraise the surprised utterances of their apprentice Hesiod.

None of the poets included here stopped at apprenticeship: no Chattertons or Shelleys, but as with the ancient Greeks these writers saw pretty much the Biblical span, apart from Dylan and Edward Thomas, and even they were already into their middle years when they died, one of personal and one of historical excesses. At the core of this book are poets who valued one another's work. David Wright was a kind of lynch-pin for several of them: C.H. Sisson, W.S. Graham and George Barker all valued him as a reader and editor. He, in turn, attentively valued the poetry of both Thomases, of Robert Graves, Lawrence Durrell and Thomas Blackburn. One of the best critics of the poetry of David Gascoyne was C.H. Sisson, who was in the habit of sending poems to Wright for appraisal before he let them appear in print. Elizabeth Smart was herself a muse; and Anne Ridler, as a significant poetry editor at Faber and Faber, a muse in another sense. Harold Pinter has been a vigorous and consistent advocate of the work of some of these writers.

This book reveals that a muse can come in a variety of forms: a novelist, an editor, an archaeologist, a nurse, a painter, a publisher, a home-maker, a historian; any one of these vocations is compatible with musedom, so long as the right poet can be found. Nothing short of detailed biography, however, can reveal the amount of patience, love and forbearance that go into the human relationships which sustain and nurture writing. A muse inspires but is also, often, self-effacing and in the end effaced, erased. Against such erasures Anthony Astbury's book of poets and muses is a revealing act of restitution and a complementary vision of some of the best British poetry from that least classical, the twentieth, century.

2005   MICHAEL SCHMIDT

Poems by

GEORGE BARKER

Selected by

ELSPETH BARKER

Elspeth, George, Bruddy, Baba and Progles. Also the donkeys,
Flower and Tilda, *c*. February 1970

FOREWORD

George was the first poet to be chosen for a selection by Greville Press in 1975, and it is an honour and a pleasure now to make this choice.

I hope that the poems here reflect the range of his voice and its development over sixty years of writing in a diversity of moods and landscapes. To me, George is vividly present in all his work, and perhaps most powerfully in the last two poems, one written for children, the other in hospital, shortly before his death.

May 2004   ELSPETH BARKER

This selection is dedicated to the memory of Margaret Elizabeth Griffiths. We, the family, are grateful to Elspeth Barker for allowing us to use her late husband's poems in this way. Margaret loved poetry and very much enjoyed meeting George on a number of occasions at Emscote Lawn Arts Festivals. We believe that this is a fitting memorial to both of them.

ROBIN GRIFFITHS

Allegory of the Adolescent and the Adult

It was when weather was Arabian I went
Over the downs to Alton where winds were wounded
With flowers and swathed me with aroma, I walked
Like Saint Christopher Columbus through a sea's welter
Of gaudy ways looking for a wonder.

Who was I, who knows, no one when I started,
No more than the youth who takes longish strides,
Gay with a girl and obstreperous with strangers,
Fond of some songs, not usually stupid,
I ascend hills anticipating the strange.

Looking for a wonder I went on a Monday,
Meandering over the Alton down and moor;
When was it I went, an hour a year or more,
That Monday back, I cannot remember.
I only remember I went in a gay mood.

Hollyhock here and rock and rose there were,
I wound among them knowing they were no wonder;
And the bird with a worm and the fox in a wood
Went flying and flurrying in front, but I was
Wanting a worse wonder, a rarer one.

So I went on expecting miraculous catastrophe.
What is it, I whispered, shall I capture a creature
A woman for a wife, or find myself a king,
Sleep and awake to find Sleep is my kingdom?
How shall I know my marvel when it comes?

Then after long striding and striving I was where
I had so long longed to be, in the world's wind,
At the hill's top, with no more ground to wander
Excepting downward, and I had found no wonder.
Found only the sorrow that I had missed my marvel.

Then I remembered, was it the bird or worm,
The hollyhock, the flower or the strong rock,
Was it the mere dream of the man and woman
Made me a marvel? It was not. It was
When on the hilltop I stood in the world's wind.

The world is my wonder, where the wind
Wanders like wind, and where the rock is
Rock. And man and woman flesh on a dream.
I look from my hill with the woods behind,
And Time, a sea's chaos, below.

Battersea Park

To Anne Ridler

Now it is November and mist wreathes the trees,
The horses cough their white blooms in the street,
Dogs shiver and boys run; the barges on the Thames
Lie like leviathans in the fog; and I meet
A world of lost wonders as I loiter in the haze
Where fog and sorrow cross my April days.

I recollect it was so often thus; with
Diamonds and pearls like mineral water pointing
The Park railings and the gardens' evergreens:
I spent my winters in summer's disappointments.
The things that burned so bright in my Augusts
Scattering me with their November dusts.

Now I marvel that I am again investigating
The fringes of the bare gardens in the winter.
I had expected to be otherwhere now,
Where the worm coils about the bone's splinter.
Now what good is the great world where I walk
That only revives desire to live once more?

How in the fog of failure and distress
Glitter of things seen in a flicker can
Paralyse will and deter determination,
Make a man afraid of the ghost of a man.
It is the wile of the world of crystal things
That catch the eye and keep me in their rings.

What I saw was Sorrow loitering along by
The Thames near the tall bridge by Battersea Park;
He had in his hand Pavlova or a swan,
And I heard him singing softly in the dark:
My twin, he sang to me, whatever of thine
Is sad and sorry, shall be glad of mine.

And he went on, singing a gay tune.
And now I know that the sorrow is this,
Not that the world a space of sorrow is
But that it's glad. O so gay a grief!
How can I ever be at home here
Where Sorrow sings of Joy in my ear?

How can I ever be happy here, where
Cock robin whistles with a gun at his breast;
Here where the flower has for bud a tear,
Here where Beauty breeds fodder for the Beast?
How can I here be happy, when I know
I can be happy only here and now?

To My Mother

Most near, most dear, most loved and most far,
Under the window where I often found her
Sitting as huge as Asia, seismic with laughter,
Gin and chicken helpless in her Irish hand,
Irresistible as Rabelais, but most tender for
The lame dogs and hurt birds that surround her, –
She is a procession no one can follow after
But be like a little dog following a brass band.

She will not glance up at the bomber, or condescend
To drop her gin and scuttle to a cellar,
But lean on the mahogany table like a mountain
Whom only faith can move, and so I send
O all my faith, and all my love to tell her
That she will move from mourning into morning.

Summer Song   I

I looked into my heart to write
    And found a desert there.
But when I looked again I heard
Howling and proud in every word
    The hyena despair.

Great summer sun, great summer sun,
    All loss burns in trophies;
And in the cold sheet of the sky
Lifelong the fish-lipped lovers lie
    Kissing catastrophes.

O loving garden where I lay
    When under the breasted tree
My son stood up behind my eyes
And groaned: Remember that the price
    Is vinegar for me.

Great summer sun, great summer sun,
    Turn back to the designer:
I would not be the one to start
The breaking day and the breaking heart
    For all the grief in China.

My one, my one, my only love,
    Hide, hide your face in a leaf,
And let the hot tear falling burn
The stupid heart that will not learn
    The everywhere of grief.

Great summer sun, great summer sun,
    Turn back to the never-never
Cloud-cuckoo, happy, far-off land
Where all the love is true love, and
    True love goes on for ever.

'Turn on your side and bear the day to me'

Turn on your side and bear the day to me
Beloved, sceptre-struck, immured
In the glass wall of sleep. Slowly
Uncloud the borealis of your eye
And show your iceberg secrets, your midnight prizes
To the green-eyed world and to me. Sin
Coils upward into thin air when you awaken
And again morning announces amnesty over
The serpent-kingdomed bed. Your mother
Watched with as dove an eye the unforgivable night
Sigh backward into innocence when you
Set a bright monument in her amorous sea.
Look down, Undine, on the trident that struck
Sons from the rock of vanity. Turn in the world
Sceptre-struck, spellbound, beloved,
Turn in the world and bear the day to me.

Galway Bay

With the gulls' hysteria above me
I walked near these breakneck seas
This morning of mists, and saw them,
Tall the mysterious queens
Waltzing in on the broad
Ballroom of the Atlantic.

All veils and waterfalls and
Wailings of the distraught,
These effigies of grief moved
Like refugees over the water;
The icy empresses of the Atlantic
Rising to bring me omen.

These women woven of ocean
And sorrows, these far sea figures,
With the fish and skull in their
Vapour of faces, the icicles
Salting down from their eyelashes,
As I walked by the foreshore

Moved towards me, ululating:
O dragnet of the sweet heart
Bind us no longer! The cage
Bursts with passions and bones,
And every highspirited fish
Lives off our scuttled love!

I stood on a stone, the gulls
Crossed my vision with wings
And my hearing with caterwauling;
The hurdling wave, backbroken,
Died at my feet. Taller
Than the towering hour above me

The homing empresses of the sea
Came among me. And, shivering,
I felt death nuzzling in the nest
Of the diurnally shipwrecked
Drowned nocturnally breast.

On a Friend's Escape From Drowning
off the Norfolk Coast

Came up that cold sea at Cromer like a running grave
    Beside him as he struck
Wildly towards the shore, but the blackcapped wave
    Crossed him and swung him back,
And he saw his son digging in the castled dirt that could save.
    Then the farewell rock
Rose a last time to his eyes. As he cried out
    A pawing gag of the sea
Smothered his cry and he sank in his own shout
    Like a dying airman. Then she
Deep near her son asleep on the hourglass sand
    Was awakened by whom
Save the Fate who knew that this was the wrong time:
    And opened her eyes
On the death of her son's begetter. Up she flies
    Into the hydra-headed
Grave as he closes his life upon her who for
    Life has so richly bedded him.
But she drove through his drowning like Orpheus and tore
    Back by the hair
Her escaping bridegroom. And on the sand their son
    Stood laughing where
He was almost an orphan. Then the three lay down
    On that cold sand,
Each holding the other by a living hand.

Roman Poem III

A Sparrow's Feather

There was this empty birdcage in the garden.
    And in it, to amuse myself, I had hung
pseudo-Oriental birds constructed of
    glass and tin bits and paper, that squeaked sadly
as the wind sometimes disturbed them. Suspended
    in melancholy disillusion they sang
of things that had never happened, and never
    could in that cage of artificial existence.
The twittering of these instruments lamenting
    their absent lives resembled threnodies
torn from a falling harp, till the cage filled with
    engineered regret like moonshining cobwebs
as these constructions grieved over not existing.
    The children fed them with flowers. A sudden gust
and without sound lifelessly one would die
    scattered in scraps like debris. The wire doors
always hung open, against their improbable
    transfiguration into, say, chaffinches
or even more colourful birds. Myself I found
    the whole game charming, let alone the children.
And then, one morning – I do not record a
    matter of cosmic proportions, I assure you,
not an event to flutter the Volscian dovecotes –
    there, askew among those constructed images
like a lost soul electing to die in Rome,
    its feverish eye transfixed, both wings fractured,
lay – I assure you, Catullus – a young sparrow.
    Not long for this world, so heavily breathing
one might have supposed this cage his destination
    after labouring past seas and holy skies
whence, death not being known there, he had flown.
    Of course, there was nothing to do. The children
brought breadcrumbs, brought water, brought tears in their
    eyes perhaps to restore him, that shivering panic
of useless feathers, that tongue-tied little gossip,
    that lying flyer. So there, among its gods
that moaned and whistled in a little wind,

flapping their paper anatomies like windmills,
wheeling and bowing dutifully to the
    divine intervention of a child's forefinger,
there, at rest and at peace among its monstrous
    idols, the little bird died. And, for my part,
I hope the whole unimportant affair is
    quickly forgotten. The analogies are too trite.

At Thurgarton Church

To the memory of my father

At Thurgarton Church the sun
burns the winter clouds over
the gaunt Danish stone
and thatched reeds that cover
the barest chapel I know.

I could compare it with
the Norse longboats that bore
burning the body forth
in honour from the shore
of great fjords long ago.

The sky is red and cold
overhead, and three small
sturdy trees keep a hold
on the world and the stone wall
that encloses the dead below.

I enter and find I stand
in a great barn, bleak and bare.
Like ice the winter ghosts and
the white walls gleam and flare
and flame as the sun drops low.

And I see, then, that slowly
the December day has gone.
I stand in the silence, not wholly
believing I am alone.
Somehow I cannot go.

Then a small wind rose, and the trees
began to crackle and stir
and I watched the moon by degrees
ascend in the window till her
light cut a wing in the shadow.

I thought: the House of the Dead.
The dead moon inherits it.
And I seem in a sense to have died
as I rise from where I sit
and out into darkness go.

I know as I leave I shall pass
where Thurgarton's dead lie
at those old stones in the grass
under the cold moon's eye.
I see the old bones glow.

No, they do not sleep here
in the long holy night of
the serene soul, but keep here
a dark tenancy and the right of
rising up to go.

Here the owl and soul shriek with
the voice of the dead as they turn
on the polar spit and burn
without hope and seek with
out hope the holy home below.

Yet to them the mole and
mouse bring a wreath and a breath
of the flowering leaves of the soul, and
it is from the Tree of Death
the leaves of life grow.

The rain, the sometime summer
rain on a memory of roses
will fall lightly and come a-
mong them as it erases
summers so long ago.

And the voices of those
once so much loved will flitter
over the nettled rows
of graves, and the holly tree twitter
like friends they used to know.

And not far away the
icy and paralysed stream
has found it also, that day the
flesh became glass and a dream
with no where to go.

Haunting the December
fields their bitter lives
entreat us to remember
the lost spirit that grieves
over these fields like a scarecrow.

That grieves over all it ever
did and all, all not
done, that grieves over
its crosspurposed lot:
to know and not to know.

The masterless dog sits
outside the church door
with dereliction haunting its
heart that hankers for
the hand that it loved so.

Not in a small grave
outside the stone wall
will the love that it gave
ever be returned, not for all
time or tracks in the snow.

More mourned the death of the dog
than our bones ever shall
receive from the hand of god
this bone again, or all
that high hand could bestow.

As I stand by the porch
I believe that no one has heard
here in Thurgarton Church
a single veritable word
save the unspoken No.

The godfathered negative
that responds to our mistaken
incredulous and heartbroken
desire above all to live
as though things were not so.

Desire to live as though the
two-footed clay stood up
proud never to know the
tempests that rage in the cup
under a rainbow.

Desire above all to live
as though the soul was stone,
believing we cannot give
or love since we are alone
and always will be so.

That heartbroken desire
to live as though no light
ever set the seas on fire
and no sun burned at night
or Mercy walked to and fro.

The proud flesh cries: I am not
caught up in the great cloud
of my unknowing. But that
proud flesh has endowed
us with the cloud we know.

To this the unspoken No
of the dead god responds
and then the whirlwinds blow
over all things and beyond
and the dead mop and mow.

And there in the livid dust
and bones of death we search
until we find as we must
outside Thurgarton Church
only wild grasses blow.

I hear the old bone in me cry
and the dying spirit call:
I have forfeited all
and once and for all must die
and this is all that I know.

For now in a wild way we
know that Justice is served
and that we die in the clay we
dread, desired, and deserved,
awaiting no Judgement Day.

Morning in Norfolk

As it has for so long
come wind and all weather
the house glimmers among
the mists of a little
river that splinters, it
seems, a landscape of
winter dreams. In the far
fields stand a few
bare trees decorating
those mists like the fanned
patterns of Georgian
skylights. The home land
of any heart persists

there, suffused with
memories and mists not
quite concealing the
identities and lost
lives of those loved once
but loved most. They haunt it
still. To the watermeadows
that lie by the heart they
return as do flocks of swallows
to the fields they have known
and flickered and flown so
often and so unforgettably over.
What fish
play in the bright wishing
wells of your painted
stretches, O secret
untainted little Bure,
I could easily tell,
for would they not be
those flashing dashers
the sometimes glittering
presentiments, images
and idealizations
of what had to be?
The dawn has brightened the
shallows and shadows and
the Bure sidles and idles
through weed isles and fallen
willows, and under
Itteringham Mill, and
there is a kind of rain-
drenched flittering in the
air, the night swan still
sleeps in her wings and over it all
the dawn heaps up the hanging
fire of the day.

Fowell's tractor blusters
out of its shed and drags
a day's work, like a piled sled
behind it. The crimson
December morning brims over

Norfolk, turning
to burning Turner
this aqueous water colour
idyll that earlier gleamed
so green that it seemed
drowned. What further
sanction, what blessing
can the man of heart intercede for
than the supreme remission
of dawn? For then the mind
looking backward upon its
too sullied yesterday,
that rotting stack of
resolution and refuse,
reads in the rainbowed sky
a greater covenant,
the tremendous pronouncement:
the day forgives.

Holy the heart in
its proper occupation
praising and appraising this
godsend, the dawn.
Will you lift up your eyes
my blind spirit and see
such evidence of
forgiveness in the heavens
morning after golden
morning that even
the blind can see?

from *Villa Stellar*

I

Why the white oxen? Simply because they are gone.
May they haunt the bright springs of Clitumnus for ever.
But I too have watched their delicate lolloping into
and out of those marzipan springs welling up like the melting of
                                                                rainbows
among emerald meadows painted afresh every morning
and seen Renoir's blood drip from their horns in the evening
and known that I was not dreaming. Now they are really gone.
                                                                Only
the proprietor's dog sleeps outside the café at noonday
and I speak in vain for the dead. The small temple so plainly
forgotten a mile further down the new highway
that in the rain a long distance lorry driver idly
supposes it nothing better than a derelict public lavatory,
there, there a dead friend and I sat sipping Frascati together
and watched the great white bullocks unwinding ribbons
of water like rainbows from around their ankles, and we know
                                                        when we see
the funeral phantasmagoria of what will never return.
So may the great white oxhead that sleeps undisturbed by even
Propertius or the susurration of a hundred poplar trees in the
                                                                evening
haunt these springs of Clitumnus for ever.

LVIII

The children are gone. The holiday is over.
Outside it is Fall. Inside it is so
quiet that the silence seems inclined to
talk to itself. They will not recover
the summer of seventy-seven again, even
though they become, in turn, their own children.

I sit in my sixty odd years and wonder
how often before in this old house a man has
sat thinking of what is now, and what was.
But can it serve a serious purpose to ponder
upon the imponderable? There, there beyond a
fall glimmers the long-lost garden.

That garden where we, too, as in a spell
stared eye into dazed eye and did not see
that suddenly the holy day was over,
the flashing lifeguard, the worm in the tree,
the glittering of the bright sword as it fell,
and the gate closing for all time to be.

A Version of Animula Vagula Blandula

I know where you are now. But do you know?
Are you here in this word? I have not heard
you whistling in the dark. Do not allow
the noun or pronoun or the verb to disturb you.
Sometimes, I think that death is really no joke
but then I have died only two or three such times.
Perhaps there is always someone to attend the
absconding mountebank. But you, farewelling ghost, poor
imperial little thing, go you alone?
Go you alone to the altering? Or am I with you?

'For a Child'

Poems by

THOMAS BLACKBURN

Selected by

JULIA BLACKBURN

Julia and Thomas Blackburn

When

What terror, what sudden dread;
A mad man wakes in his straw;
Cold, sweating, upright in bed,
A child wakes and watches his door,
As from his cellarage
A mad man climbs up a stair.

But the lunatic cannot come in
To the room of the haunted child.
O, when will it come about,
Eyes skinned so he understand,
That a child, upright, unafraid,
Take a blind, mad man by the hand?

Exorcism of Ghosts

The exorcism of ghosts in the night by a tree,
In a bed in the room of a house where they were alone
And the terror far more than they could bear or understand,
Is a child reading his parents' graveyard stone
And the lives of the dead on the palm of his hand.

The anguish of ghosts in the dark by a poisonous tree,
Of a girl by a stream and a man in his bed in the dark,
Is now in the dark as the stream, the bed and the tree;
Cold as the stream, hard as the bed and cruel as the tree.

The exorcism of ghosts is the mind of a child.
They come from the dark to the door of his mind
And listen to words they never knew how to say,
The thought of their child is a light in the dark
And his search is a path for ghosts who have lost their way.

The child shall have need of the ghost and the ghost of the child,
They shall bend to the narrow wall of skin and bone,
Dividing the quick and the dead, till a cock crows
And all come praising out of the haunted stone.

Prayer for the Unborn Children

Prayer of the night of the unborn children
Dying into the night of their becoming birth,
Born into the iron of the terrible night
Of the dream that is waiting for the unborn children over all the
           earth.

Prayer for the newborn children crying
In the folds of the skin of the beast of their world.
For the ghost in the ice of the breast,
For the words, words settling on the children like enormous birds.

Cold of the bone of the hand on the child
Crying in the cage of the small room for the wide ghost.
To the great ghost of the child dying
In the mask of the lost in the room of the dark of the child crying.

Prayer of the ghost for the child,
Becoming the child. The prayer of the ghost for the room,
For the child, the hand and the breast,
The prayer of the ghost.
The prayer of the lost for the ghost for the child,
The prayer of the ghost in the child for the lost,
The prayer of the Ghost.

Last Night

Last night came crying into my breast
Like a child from the stone chest
Of some attic room, my pristine fear.
I was brought down low again and pressed near
Its buried life. Child, child,
It seems that you did not die;
Now, in the founded house of middle age,
Open my lips and utter your piercing cry,
On the nursery floor of the heart,
Weep, weep and rage.

The Unpredictable

The raw and overwhelming danger
Of the first grief and the first hunger,
Too much, I dare say, to be caught
By a child's heartbeat and his thought.

Mercifully, though, from too much violence
There is oblivion and silence,
Postponing love and the great anger,
For latter days when we are stronger.

But to go round and round again
In a dead dream of dead men,
From the stopped heart and the checked word;
This also has occurred,

And tall constructions from a first
Unquenched and undiminished thirst,
Out of weakness and much danger,
The laurel crown, the hero's posture.

To have suffered, though, to have done
With the black light of the first sun,
Though the drink's stale, the bread putrid,
This is beyond love and hatred;

To have worked out, to exceed
The Furies and the human need,
Is unpredictable, a grace
Of no time, no place.

An Aftermath

They hadn't noticed her coming, too busy with loud
Out-goings, that savage night, his wife and he;
Two's company, you know, but three's a crowd,
And the upthrust and draught of fantasy
Leave little room a child can hope to fill.
Evil each saw and nothing else could see,
The two of them were dead if looks could kill;
And then they turned and saw her balanced there
Upon the spinning rim of their nightmare.

I'd like to think it shook them to a pause,
Their daughter, her shut face, but that's not true;
Nothing mattered to them but an antique ghost,
And the open rent in their sides it cackled through.
One can imagine what sly words they said
To shrug the violence off and half explain
A foundered world, then pack her off to bed;
Speed was what counted, they'd to fight again
Within a ring they tried to think their own –
Making the darkness where she lay alone.

Such smilings, though, on the morning after that night!
Red-handed both of them, they groped for chat –
It's easy to make darkness but not light –
He pointed out the business of some cat,
There on the lawn, the feathers of a bird,
But knew she knew the game that they'd been at:
Those burnt out eyes of her had never stirred
From what between them in the night occurred.

'A door,' he murmured, 'a door bruised mother's eye?'
She stared of course clean through that question mark,
Puzzled he'd offered her a half-baked lie.
Like cats, he thought, a child sees through the dark,
And, with no adult technique of escape,
Runs the bad gauntlet of its parents' dream:
What is a fitting panacea for rape?
Strawberries I think they offered and whipped cream;
Within that garden where the shapes of night
Still prowled about them in the June sunlight.

As bedtime came, he sensed her terror grow;
Would it rise again, the petroleum sea, and pluck
Their features away in its savage undertow;
Must she ride their beaten minds down gulfs of shock?
She undergoes, he thought, what we've undergone –
Remembering, himself a child, how the house would rock –
Will this circle of revenants never, never be done,
Must ever the haunted ones to haunt come back?
He turned and saw his daughter was asleep,
His wife beside her in the faint blue air;
It seems as well as furies of the deep,
Moments of clarity we also share.

The Drummer

For Erica Marx

He knelt beyond the wood and said,
'I had a child, as white as snow
Her skin, her lips as red as blood,
But oh, that dark corrosive flood;
The drumstick and the drummer.'

Over the turf the drummer came
And lifted up his hollow bone
And brought the wicked drumsticks down,
'Everything is lost and gone
But my rap rap rapping tune;
The drumstick and the drummer.'

'I curse your tune,' the mourner said,
'Which stole the dayspring from my heart
And stopped her breath and froze each vein
So that we two now lie apart
And chaos rumbles down again,'
But over his imploring breath
The drummer raised his wagging bone
And brought the wicked drumsticks down,
Where has all that sweetness gone?
The drumstick and the drummer.

Then from his knees he leapt and stood
Bolt upright by the drumming man,
And cracked his knuckle-bones and laughed,
'We are neither here nor there
But the passion of this tune.'
Through his fingers, sopped in blood,
Roared the drumbeats burning down
All their sad and mortal clay.

The mourner and the drumming man
Beat their circumstance away,
'Everything is lost,' they sang,
'But our rap rap rapping tune,
The drumstick and the drummer.'

A Smell of Burning

After each savage, hysterical episode,
So common with us, my mother would sniff the air
And murmur, 'Nurse, would you look at the upstairs fire,
I smell burning, something's alight somewhere.'
But a red coal never was found, or jet of gas,
Scorching dry board, or paint-work beginning to melt;
And too young was I in that nursery time to guess
What smoking, subjective fire she really smelt.
Nowadays I know quite well from hers they came,
And my father's mouth, when the hot tongues crackled and spat;
But what mattered then was a trick of dodging flame,
And keeping some breath alive in the heat of it.
I have it still that inbred dodging trick;
But always – when fire beset – I see them turning,
My parents, to name elsewhere their sour fire reek,
And touch myself and know what's really burning.

Oedipus

His shadow monstrous on the palace wall.
That swollen boy, fresh from his mother's arms,
The odour of her body on his palms,
Moves to the eyeless horror of the hall.

And with what certainty the Revelation
Gropes for the sage's lips; words whine and bark
Out of that crumpled linen in the dark
To name the extremity of violation.

How should he not but tremble as the world
Contracts about him to his mother's room,
Red-curtained, stifling; in the firelit gloom
His swollen manhood on her bed is curled.

Then up and blind him, hands, pull blackness down
And let this woman on the strangling cord,
Hang in the rich embroidery of her gown;
Then up and blind him, pull the blackness down.

But as he stumbles to the desert sands,
Bleeding and helpless as the newly born,
His daughters leading him with childish hands,
I see beyond all words his future shape,
Its feet upon the carcass of the ape
And round its mighty head, prophetic birds.

By the Water

To the place where of late lay her numinous darlings,
As grey as the evening, she hugged a wet stone,
And railed at, knee deep in the river of weeping,
The waters where all her tall children had gone.

'Oh, bring back my daughters from under the waters,
My sons of the ivy and holy bay-tree,
You sundering, blundering river of darkness
Who wash down my loves to the ignorant sea.

With vine leaves o'erladen, both harlot and maiden,
They shook a wild blood from the heart of the world,
As sleepers advancing to join their proud dancing,
Their streamers of daylight from midnight unfurled.

Ah, now they are caught in the shops they are bought in,
And measure their weight in a rattle-ing mart;
Pinned out with neat labels on accurate tables,
Those children who grew from the roots of my heart.'

Alone and un-mighty the Queen Aphrodite
Stood shorn of her brilliants and haggard and grey,
The mute sea lay sleeping, the woman was weeping,
Her arms round a stone she had plucked from the bay.

'Oh bring back my daughters,' she cried to the waters,
'My sons of the ivy, and holy bay-tree,
Let harlot and maiden with vine leaves o'erladen,
Come back to my heart from the caves of the sea.'

In the Fire

When they saw how to the fire
All and everything was brought,
How the tongue and eyes and hands
Lit and dwindled and burnt out,
Naked of their mortal dream,
Tallow man and woman lay,
Watching how the wicks of time
Ate their married flesh away.
Finding nothing they found all,
Who had thought the blood might prove,
In a mingled circumstance,
Some equation for their love.
As the place their bodies sought
Dwindled into wisps of air,
Lonely in the muscled dark,
He and she were pardoned where
Cloudy distances grew large
In between them on their bed;
So each baffled spirit found
Nothing of its ghostliness
To mortality was bound.
When they saw how to the fire
All and everything was brought,
Such a freedom rinsed and sang
Through their wild, uncreatured thought,
Separate man and woman lay
Praising as the wicks of time
Burnt their circumstance away.

Hospital for Defectives

By your unnumbered charities
A miracle disclose,
Lord of the Images, whose love,
The eyelid and the rose
Takes for a language, and today
Tell to me what is said
By these men in a turnip field
And their unleavened bread.

For all things seem to figure out
The stirrings of your heart,
And two men pick the turnips up
And two men pull the cart;
And yet between the four of them
No word is ever said
Because the yeast was not put in
Which makes the human bread.
But three men stare on vacancy
And one man strokes his knees;
What is the meaning to be found
In such dark vowels as these?

Lord of the Images, whose love,
The eyelid and the rose
Takes for a metaphor, today
Beneath the warder's blows,
The unleavened man did not cry out
Or turn his face away;
Through such men in a turnip field
What is it that you say?

For a Child

And have I put upon your shoulders then,
What in myself I have refused to bear,
My own and the confusion of dead men,
You of all these, my daughter, made my heir,
The furies and the griefs of which I stayed
Quite unaware?

Perhaps because I did not with my tongue
State these sharp energies into the mind,
They are the shadows you grow up among;
You suffer darkness because I was blind,
Take up the chaoses that in myself
Were unconfined.

If I should say, I also know the tart
Flavour of other men, as my excuse,
And took into myself their broken heart,
That's not the point, abuse remains abuse;
May chaos though have light within your mind,
And be of use.

Mercy

With her sailor hat and her kitten
Tucked in a coat and warm,
You, will You keep my daughter
From any particular harm?
I mean because of the habit
Of love, and the way she has
Of leaning upon the shoulder
Of this bent world of Yours,
As if she feared no disaster
Wound in the skein of the years,
No beaten man or woman
Crawling upon all fours,
But trusted whatever happens
Is destined to occur;
If You have need of mercy,
God, have mercy on her.

The Sediment

One step, it takes almost a minute now
Those stiffening arteries won't let blood through,
What next, I wonder, as I take your arm
And guide across a floor what's left of you;
Eyesight perhaps, the breath and then the heart,
Yes, that will do.

But must he bear this upright quivering?
'Wheel-chair,' I say; the nurse, 'He'd give up hope.'
Sans teeth, sans eyes, sans taste, sans everything?
I watch her getting busy with the soap,
Details still matter (choir where no birds sing)
But who'd have thought death needed so much rope.
'Have a good night,' she says, 'you've but to ring . . .'
And then the dope.

It's like incoming, though, this going out.
It seemed to me this morning that your breath
And bubbling lips upon a milky spout
Were reminiscent both of birth and death,
And as I watch the working of your jaws,
I do not think I've seen you less perplexed,
Less needing approbation and applause,
My father, than turned here, unmanned and sexed,
Towards your cause.

But it's not true to say, 'all passion spent'.
Into a glare, removed and murmuring,
Quite undiminished by your charred event,
You lapsed last night, as if this perishing
Fell from yourself in grains, mere sediment:
Let no one to the marriage of true minds
Admit impediment.

Mental Ward

They shall be new at the roots of their sane trees
After the various drugs to ward off disaster,
They shall drift down like birds from the high fells
To the boles of the trees where no one is a stranger.

They shall celebrate their union with each other,
Men and women, speechless in life, dumb as the roots of trees,
In good communion of talk and laughter
And prove they are found now who had lost their ways.

For these are those who in the parish of living,
Having no good instrument on which to play,
Still worked hard and with the almost nothing
Of their scant tongue and brain on the great symphony.

The man who barked like a dog shall talk of angels.
The girl, so far gone, no skill could disinter
Her buried soul, in superb parabolas
Of dance and song celebrate the life in her.

There shall be no more desolation or crying anywhere.

For the great pianist who strummed on one string
With a broken finger, shall have an infinity of chords,
And the stopped poet who could only say 'Good morning',
Reap with his tongue a harvest of meaningful words.

They shall be written in the centre of the page
Who were in parenthesis here,
For withdrawn from the body which held them in close siege
There shall be no more desolation anywhere.

No more desolation anywhere.

Kinder Scout

For Bonamy Dobrée

Hares, on this sodden mountain,
White, surprised by the thaw,
Appear like moments of vision
Then silently melt away
Between a communion of boulders
That shape a rain washed sky.
Now water repeats to silence
The name of a running stream
And, falling, creates a presence
That lives while the stream flows on
But would die like a man from the absence
Of water, and turn to stone.

I climb to the source of the water
And watch it break from the turf –
So a child comes out of its mother
To traffic with death and life –
And know that the stream is neither
This cup where it murmurs one small
Word to the lichen and gravel,
Or its leap from that sudden fall

To a salt and tidal river,
Since just as my life exceeds
Its day of birth and dying,
This headlong water evades
The definition of boulders
That give it shape for one breath
And has a purpose such details
Are not familiar with.
Darkness covers the mountain;
Why must we travel this way
Over hags of peat and boulders?
That I shall never know,
But hares, like moments of vision,
Run white and then melt away.

Trewarmett

For Julia Blackburn

Darkness, feathers are shed;
These birds are gathered back
By the enormous hand
That cast them at dawn seaward
In crumbs of living bread
To their forefathering rock.

Piercing the lens of a wave,
From the beat of it and the swell,
The feathered life they have
Is indivisible,
As from the undertow
And skin of a nervous sea
Fish and themselves also
They reap perpetually.
Being clothed, and without a seam,
In the pouring waters they thread,
How can they miss their aim,
By the loose surge targeted
Forever towards their home?

Darkness, feathers are shed;
From this bird-whitened stone,
I watch a cormorant pluck
Life from a nervous sea,
With a moon behind my back,
Conscious of God knows what
Anxious irrelevance
As these birds swim in the eye
Of the green circumstance
From which I am undone
By my duplicity.

Watching a bird, and a man
Watching a bird in the surf,
Watched by a man, and that faint
Rim of horizon far off
Where darkness breeds from a glint
Of metal, I wait for the tide
To work its equation out.
Though hunger, compulsive dread,
Are ghosts forever unlaid
By a moon's impetus
That takes the sea by the throat,
I assert, as it gathers up all
Of night to one moment of stress
That is perpetual,
My own self-consciousness.
The waters boom and rave;
Being human, what else can I have
Than such good and growing pain,
Between the living and dead,
On this sea-shaken stone?

Laudate

There the sea birds come at first light in all weathers, on all days,
To a particular field for feeding, feathered in the sun's faint rays,
And through sleep I still catch their sea cries,
Turning my dreams to ocean themes whose great rhythm never
dies,
Think of cliffs of sleep till some great hand sends the birds on
their highways,
Draws them back when it is evening to the coigns above the bays;
Master hand that with a difference on our human being plays
And will never let us fall, for death as an end is a pack of lies,
This the wind that blows at midnight to the stars above us says,
Age is but a growing nearer to being without what flesh purveys
So however bad the weather what is there to do but praise.

Morituri

Such beatitudes of water
Where the scree falls to the sand
In the August sun they glitter
One might think world without end,
But tomorrow the sun may be dark and
The waters running with foam,
But it's all a grace and a Godsend
And the exile's going home.

Blake said the vegetable copy
Of eternity this world is,
There humans and flowers and the oak-tree
Shall shine with intensities,
This mundane shell the five senses
Curtails. In death sensuality
Shall enlarge and distances
And nearnesses we shall see
As they really are if the stress
Is endured; we are born to suffer,
So blessed we learn to bless.

An Epitaph

By much speaking I fled from silence,
To many friends from the one stranger,
By food and drink I cheated hunger,
And by meek words, abuse and violence.

My loss increased as I grew richer,
My load more great with lighter burden,
With less guilt, more sought I pardon.
As light flowered, I grew blinder.

I quenched my thirst by lack of water,
And found myself where I was absent,
Faith half I proved by the inconstant
Moon: truth because I was a liar.

Now far still from the heart's centre,
But with less storm, less crying,
I wait for birth again, now dying
Has opened its door and let me enter.

'Too Far to Hear the Singing'

Poems by

LAWRENCE DURRELL

Selected by

FRANÇOISE KESTSMAN DURRELL

Far out on the blue
Like notes of music on a page
The two heads: the man and his wife.
They are always there.

It is too far to hear the singing.
From 'Matapan' (1943)

Françoise Kestsman Durrell and Lawrence Durrell, Sommières, 1987

FOREWORD

Sometimes it happens to me to wonder where Larry's mind could be nowadays. And more and more frequently. I don't know why, but perhaps because solitude is very often too much heavy to afford. The only way to feel in touch with the companion of my closeself is to listen to music or better to read poetry, Larry's of course. But, as everybody knows, poetry is the music of the soul. That is my way to feel Larry coming back and one more time, in osmosis with him.

2005   F.K.D.

Highwayman

The road is a sinister pathway paved with smoke,
A faint, white tremor; in the encircling trees
Grow the little whispers, oak to friendly oak,
Sentinels of the road.
                  Darker than these
Full in the shadow of the leaning elm
A restive horse pads on the level grass,
And counts the seconds; dark, immobile sits
The masked rider, gleaming oblique slits
For eyes, watching the timid minutes pass
On stealthy feet, hurrying the approach
Of time;
           Far out upon the curving road
Glitters, an unsuspecting prey, the Midnight Coach…

1931

from *Cities, Plains and People*

Beirut 1943

I

Once in idleness was my beginning,

Night was to the mortal boy
Innocent of surface like a new mind
Upon whose edges once he walked
In idleness, in perfect idleness.

O world of little mirrors in the light.
The sun's rough wick for everybody's day:
Saw the Himalayas like lambs there
Stir their huge joints and lay
Against his innocent thigh a stony thigh.

Combs of wind drew through this grass
To bushes and pure lakes
On this tasteless wind
Went leopards, feathers fell or flew:
Yet all went north with the prayer-wheel,
By the road, the quotation of nightingales.

Quick of sympathy with springs
Where the stone gushed water
Women made their water like thieves.

Caravans paused here to drink Tibet.
On draughty corridors to Lhasa
Was my first school
In faces lifted from saddles to the snows:
Words caught by the soft klaxons crying
Down to the plains and settled cities.

So once in idleness was my beginning.
Little known of better then or worse
But in the lens of this great patience
Sex was small,
Death was small,
Were qualities held in a deathless essence,
Yet subjects of the wheel, burned clear
And immortal to my seventh year.

To all who turn and start descending
The long sad river of their growth:
The tidebound, tepid, causeless
Continuum of terrors in the spirit,
I give you here unending
In idleness an innocent beginning

Until your pain become a literature.

1946

Song for Zarathustra

Le saltimbanque is coming with
His heels behind his head.
His smile is mortuary and
His whole expression dead.

The acrobat, the acrobat,
Demanding since the Fall
Little enough but hempen stuff
To climb and hang us all.

Mysterious inventions like
The trousers and the hat
Bewitched our real intentions:
We sewed the fig-leaves flat.

Man sewed his seven pockets
Upon his hairy clothes
But woman in her own white flesh
Has one she seldom shows.

An aperture on anguish,
A keyhole on disgrace:
The features stay grimacing
Upon the mossy face.

A cup without a handle
A staff without a crook,
The sawdust in the golly's head,
The teapot with the nook.

The Rib is slowly waking
Within the side of Man
And *le guignol* is making
Its faces while it can.

Compose us in the finder
Our organs upside down,
The parson in his widow's weeds,
The doctor in his gown.

What Yang and Yin divided
In one disastrous blunder
Must one day be united and
Let no man put asunder.

1948

Sarajevo

Bosnia. November. And the mountain roads
Earthbound but matching perfectly these long
And passionate self-communings counter-march,
Balanced on scarps of trap, ramble or blunder
Over traverses of cloud: and here they move,
Mule-teams like insects harnessed by a bell
Upon the leaf-edge of a winter sky,

And down at last into this lap of stone
Between four cataracts of rock: a town
Peopled by sleepy eagles, whispering only
Of the sunburnt herdsman's hopeless ploy:
A sterile earth quickened by shards of rock
Where nothing grows, not even in his sleep,

Where minarets have twisted up like sugar
And a river, curdled with blond ice, drives on
Tinkling among the mule-teams and the mountaineers,
Under the bridges and the wooden trellises
Which tame the air and promise us a peace
Harmless with nightingales. None are singing now.

No history much? Perhaps. Only this ominous
Dark beauty flowering under veils,
Trapped in the spectrum of a dying style:
A village like an instinct left to rust,
Composed around the echo of a pistol-shot.

1951

The Octagon Room

1955

Veronese grey! Here in the Octagon Room
Our light ruffles and decodes
Greys of cigar-ash or river clay
Into the textual plumage of a mind –
Paulo, all his Muses held
Quietly in emulsion up against
A pane of cockney sky.

It is not only the authority
Of godly sensual forms which pity
And overwhelm us – this grey copied
From eyes I no more see,
Recording every shade of pain, yes,
All it takes to give smiles
The deathly candour of a dying art,
Or worth to words exchanged in darkness:
Is it only the dead who have such eyes?

No, really,
I think it is the feudal calm
Of sensuality enjoyed without aversion
Or regret… (incident of the ring
Lost in the grass: her laughter).

I should have been happy
In these rainy streets, a captive still
Like all these glittering hostages
We carried out of Italy, canvases
Riding the cracking winds in great London
Parks: happy or unhappy, who can tell you?

Only Veronese grey walks backwards
In the past across my mind
To where tugs still howl and mumble
On the father river,
And the grey feet passing, quiver
On pavements greyer than his greys…

Less wounding perhaps because the belongers
Loved here, died here, and took their art
Like love, with a pinch of salt, yes
Their pain clutched in the speechless
Deathless calm of Method. Gods!

1956

Eleusis

With dusk rides up the god-elated night,
Perfume of goatskin and footsore stone
Where plants expire in chaff and husk
On marble threshing-floors of bone.

Here in the gallery where the initiates strained
To lick the sacred ribbon from the soil,
Still wet from the libation's stains of
Honey, grain and this year's olive-oil.

Well: to sit down, to anonymise a bit
By some unleavened altar which preserves
An echo of truth for the precocious will,
Of some disinherited science of the nerves.

'How long will the full Unlearning take?
How long the unacting and unthinking run?
When does the obelisk the sleeper wake
Repaired and newly minted like a sun?'

'The issues change, alas the problems never.
The capital question cuts to the very bone.
Drink here your draught of the eternal fever,
Sit down unthinking on the Unwishing stone.'

1961

The Ikons

They have taken another road,
Dionysus and all his cockledom,
The ogres in dry river beds
Hair flying, breast-bone full of eyes.
A madman walks alone in the dark wood
Swinging a lantern; nobodies march,
Lute-player, card-sharper, politician,
Until here lastly the condign
Majestic stance of something else
Apparelled for death: Byzantium.

The eyes won't change, no, but the
Going forward or going back
Can be read off as on a clock-face.
Here the population of clocks multiplied,
They bore the suffocating fruits of chime, hours.
All day long the belfries reminded
All night the prayers besieged.
A cross rose, wish-bone of the defeated,
The chicken-souled, the guilty.
It has got worse since, of course,
And can hardly get any better now.

A café is the last Museum and best,
To observe a great man in the middle
Of a collapse; but parts work still,
The crutches are incidental, adding variety.
Some injudicious pleasures will remain,
The sexual phosphorescence of youth is gone,
But here on naphtha-scented evenings still
He sits before the tulip of old wine,
In a red fez, by some sunken garden,
Watching for shooting-stars.

1966

The Outer Limits

The pure form, then, must be the silence?
I'd tear out a leaf of it and spread it,
The second skin of music, yes,
And with a drypoint then etch in quick
Everything that won't talk back, like
Frost or rain or the budget of spring:
Even some profligate look or profitable
Embrace – here to imprison it,
So full of a gay informal logic,
A real reality realising itself,
No pressures but candid as a death,
A full foreknowledge of the breathing game
Taut as a bent bow the one simple life
Too soon over, too soon cold; memory
Will combine for you voice, odour, smile.

1968

Feria: Nîmes

Feria; cloaked trigonometry of hooves
The plane trees know, shiver with apprehension;
They plead as the archons of the blue steel must
These prayers, refining murder by a breath,
Turn self-deception to an absolution –
Two coloured pawns uniting in the rites of death.

Brocade still stiff with bloody hair he kneels
While the mithraic sun sinks in a surf
Of bloody bubbles; leaks from the huge pizzle
The holy urine smoking in the dust.
He reels into a darkness which he dazzles.

Tall doors fall as the axes must,
And the great sideboard of the bull is there,
A landslide in the ordinary heart
A feast for gods within a coat of hair,
His thunder like a belfry and his roars
The minotaur of man's perfected lust,
His birth-pangs offered to the steel's applause.

1990

Le cercle refermé

Boom of the sunset gun
In the old fortress at Benares,
And a single sobbing bugle calls
The naphtha flares on river craft
Corpses floating skyward
The thumbworship of the dead
Gnomes with their vast collisions
Of water and weed and light
With the dead awake all night
The coffined dead true in love's despite
The thumbscrews of awareness screwed in tight.

The girl with nine wombs is there to chide
What does it mean, your ancient loneliness?
Today they are coming to measure me for a coffin,
So dying you begin to sleepwalk and regain your youth.

Mere time is winding down at last:
The consenting harvest moon presides,
Appears on cue to hold our hearts in fee,
The genetics of our doubts holds fast
And a carotid is haunted by old caresses
The caresses of silence.
When young and big with poems
Caressed by my heliocentric muse
With lunar leanings, I was crafty in loving,
Or jounty as a god of the bullfrogs
The uncanny promptings of the human I.

Love-babies nourished by the sigh,
With little thought of joy or pain,
Or the spicy Kodak of the hangman's brain
A disenfranchised last goodbye,
                              Goodbye.

                                                        1990

Poems by

DAVID GASCOYNE

Selected by

JUDY GASCOYNE

David and Judy Gascoyne

FOREWORD

I would like to thank Tony for giving me a chance to choose some of David's poems that have meant so much to me.

Most friends know how we met at the Island Psychiatric Hospital where I was reading poetry to severely depressed patients. When I chose to read 'September Sun' to the class, I was surprised when a tall, sad looking man told me he was David Gascoyne and he had written the poem. I wasn't sure whether to believe him but, over a cup of tea, he convinced me.

A friendship developed when David spent most weekends at my house. My husband was having an affair and I was feeling sad too! Then David and I had a week in London due to an unexpected cheque from the Royal Literary Fund. There, David was a different person amongst his old friends, and visits to art galleries and concerts were a revelation with him. Back home we realised that we had fallen in love so, when my husband told me he wanted a divorce, we were able to clinch the deal as it were!

So for the next few months we were like youngsters planning our wedding. Soon I went to live at David's house near Cowes, and there life was very peaceful. David was still wanting to do nothing and I don't think I put any pressure on him. Two treats for me came up, one a garden party at Buck House because David is on the Civil List, and surprisingly we both enjoyed that. The turning point was a visit to Paris at the invitation of the British Council. Once again David was in his element, and kind friends welcomed him warmly.

It was the start of many visits to Paris, and David returning to his translating again. Gradually he began to feel better and to write an occasional poem, which I was the first to read.

When he became a committee member of the World Poetry Society, it entailed travelling the world to meet poets from every country. That kept us really busy and David didn't get much time for writing. To my amazement, he often wrote poems for special subjects when asked; and he also wrote regular obituaries when his famous old friends sadly died.

In 1994 David had a really bad fall while I was out, which needed three months in hospital, which he hated and he became seriously depressed again. For the last six years we've had much happiness, and one of the best days out was when David went in a wheelchair to receive his Chevalier award at the French Institute. Life is quieter now but, thanks to Enitharmon Press, his books of poetry and prose are published, and he seems to be more famous than ever! Not that he aspires to anything like that.

Cowes, 2001   JUDY GASCOYNE

September Sun: 1947

Magnificent strong sun! in these last days
So prodigally generous of pristine light
That's wasted only by men's sight who will not see
And by self-darkened spirits from whose night
Can rise no longer orison or praise:

Let us consume in fire unfed like yours
And may the quickened gold within me come
To mintage in due season, and not be
Transmuted to no better end than dumb
And self-sufficient usury. These days and years

May bring the sudden call to harvesting,
When if the fields Man labours only yield
Glitter and husks, then with an angrier sun may He
Who first with His gold seed the sightless field
Of Chaos planted, all our trash to cinders bring.

The Goose-Girl

She at whose feet I'll finally fall down
With all my niggardly belated offering
Of real emotion, is a lonely silent girl
Who knows no more than I about love's boon
But sits and wonders – feeling at a loss
Among the queens and conquerors who stroll
So poised and pleased about the social scene –
Waiting for no-one from an old wives' tale,
But for a childless father and her father's unborn son.

Oxford: A Spring Day

For Bill

The air shines with a mild magnificence…
Leaves, voices, glitterings… And there is also water
Winding in easy ways among much green expanse,

Or lying flat, in small floods, on the grass;
Water which in its widespread crystal holds the whole soft song
Of this swift tremulous instant of rebirth and peace.

Tremulous – yet beneath, how deep its root!
Timelessness of an afternoon! Air's gems, the walls' bland grey,
Slim spires, hope-coloured fields: these belong to no date.

1941

Rex Mundi

I heard a herald's note announce the coming of a king.

He who came sounding his approach was a small boy;
The household trumpet that he flourished a tin toy.

Then from a bench beneath the boughs that lately Spring
Had hung again with green across the avenue, I rose
To render to the king who came the homage subjects owe.

And as I waited, wondered why it was that such a few
Were standing there with me to see him pass; but understood
As soon as he came into sight, this was a monarch no
Crowds of this world can recognize, to hail him as they should.

He drove past in a carriage that was drawn by a white goat;
King of the world to come where all that shall be now is new.
Calmly he gazed on our pretentious present that is not.

Of morals, classes, business, war, this child
Knew nothing. We were pardoned when he smiled.

If you hear it in the distance, do not scorn the herald's note.

Sentimental Colloquy

Daphne: The evening in the towns when Summer's over
Has always this infectious sadness, Conrad;
And when we walk together after rain
As darkness gathers in the public gardens,
There is such hopelessness about the leaves
That now lie strewn in heaps along each side
Of the wet asphalt paths, that as we turn
Back to the gardens' closing gates, we two,
Though in our early twenties still, seem elderly,
Both of us, Conrad, quietly quite resigned
And humbled into silence by the Fall…

Conrad: My dear, even your Mother is not elderly!
A woman is a girl or an old maid.
Yet I too do feel muted by this twilight;
For as it ever is the tendency
Of dusk to fall, and of past Summer's leaves,
At this time not of day but of the year,
To drop from trees, so surely must we fall
Silent if we take lovers' strolls in Autumn
Hoping we'll not fall out before the Spring.

Daphne: I hate you, Conrad, if that's what you're hoping!
I don't believe you think I'm a 'young girl'.
There is already in the air that hint of death
That when we breathe it makes us winter-wise.

Conrad: I do not think we to ourselves appear
A pair of fledglings. Let the middle-aged
Be sentimentally aware of their maturity
But let us not seem to invite their envy.
We shall be like them sooner than we think.

Daphne:	There go a couple really bent with care:
	Oh, look! how they both love each other, though,
	In spite of –

Conrad:	Why, you only speak your wish,
	Daphne, you've not looked close enough!
	A pair of ancient fish, my love, out of the deep:
	Mute and expressionless they loom and pass
	On their dim way across the ocean floor
	Of roaring London.

Daphne:	Conrad, how long ago
	Did we sink drowned in it? Little you care
	For two such poor old phantoms. Sink or swim,
	We have no choice, since gravity descends
	And we although our love's still young
	And though true love's immortal, are as old
	And sink as fast as hearts of stone, if we pretend
	We care for no one but ourselves,
	Failing to recognize that that's who they are.

| Conrad: | You will become a Sybil, sweetheart, soon. |

November in Devon

Leaving Plymouth last seen after first smashed by bombs,
   Driving North all the morning after rain
     Towards Hartland's hospitable hearth
    Through landscapes clad in disruptive pattern
Material edged by hedge or walls of dry-stone:

Under a cover of commingling cloud and clear,
   Drifts of drab haze transpierced by wet blue slate,
     Between lofty moor and deep glen
    Past lanes twisting off into the arcane
We spin towards midday's strengthening sun.

After Launceston eleven o'clock approaches
    At a thousand revs per minute four times
        Beneath us: the car radio
    Picks up brass playing *Nimrod* in Whitehall,
Rearousing a reticent love for this land.

While memory brings back like a sepia still
    Holding my mother's hand in a Bournemouth
        Doorway during the first of all
    Remembrance Days' two minutes of silence,
Today I anticipate the advent of death.

A parade of folk sporting mass-produced poppies
    In the next village briefly delays us
        At a border-point round which spread
    Areas of age-old non-violence.
In ivy-dark gardens hang white rags of late rose.

An abrupt paranoia wonders just how sure
    One can be now that no secret convoy
        Was out during last night on roads
    Linking Hinkley Point and Bull Head, that near-
by tin-mines or tumuli hide no lethal hoards.

At half my age this might have worried me more.
    The South country kept my childhood secure.
        Now I know that to Whinny-moor
    Before long I shall come, as one more year
Declines towards departure in deceptive calm.

                                        1986

Half-an-Hour

To Meraud Guevara

… and grass grows round the door. The ground,
Without, is grained with root and stone
And yellow-stained where sunlight pours on sand
Through listlessly stirred chestnut-leaves.
This is the long-sought still retreat,
This is the house, the quiet land,
My spirit craves.

   A burning sound,
Uninterrupted as the flow of high-noon's light
Down on the trees from whence it emanates,
The song of the cigales, slowly dissolves
All other thought than that of absolute
Consent, even to anxious transience.

                           Aix-en-Provence

from *Three Venetian Nocturnes*

2   Lido Gala Fireworks

Rockets released tonight rush up to rape the grapebloom sky:
Rainbows of gelid jewellery smashed to flashlit smithereens
And moulting molten-crystal plumes of birds of paradise
Spontaneously splintering their mixed Murano tints
Into a slowly dropping drift of dust of opals, Milky Way
Stained with a long dynasty of fire-peacocks' last blood;
Till all night's spark-sprayed dome is stunned with quick
                                airquakes of gold,
Precipitous ephemerae and crepitations, streaked
With shivering scars of wounds stabbed by the rays of soaring
                                      stars,

Stars piercing scarlet holes, holes bleeding light,
Light strained through silk, silk blobbed with black,
Black blurred with sea-water, blue…

Lines

So much to tell: so measurelessly more
Than this poor rusting pen could ever dare
To try to scratch a hint of… Words are marks
That flicker through men's minds like quick black dust;
That falling, finally obliterate the faint
Glow their speech emanates. Too soon all sparks
Of vivid meaning are extinguished by
The saturated wadding of Man's tongue…
And yet, I lie, I lie:
Can even Omega discount
The startling miracle of human song?

Apologia

'Poète et non honnête homme'
Pascal

1

It's not the Age,
Disease, or accident, but sheer
Perversity (or so one must suppose),
That pins me to the singularly bare
Boards of this trestle-stage
That I have mounted to adopt the pose
Of a demented wrestler, with gorge full
Of phlegm, eyes bleared with salt, and knees
Knocking like ninepins: a most furious fool!

Fixed by the nib
Of an inept pen to a bleak page
Before the glassy gaze of a ghost mob,
I stand once more to face the silent rage
Of my unseen Opponent, and begin
The same old struggle for the doubtful prize:
Each stanza is a round, and every line
A blow aimed at the too elusive chin
Of that Oblivion which cannot fail to win.

3

Before I fall
Down silent finally, I want to make
One last attempt at utterance, and tell
How my absurd desire was to compose
A single poem with my mental eyes
Wide open, and without even one lapse
From that most scrupulous Truth which I pursue
When not pursuing Poetry. – Perhaps
Only the poem I can never write is *true*.

Odeur de Pensée

Thought has a subtle odour: which is not
Like that which hawthorn after rainfall has;
Nor is it sickly or astringent as
Are some scents which round human bodies float,
Diluting sweat's thick auras. It's not like
Dust's immemorial smells, which lurk
Where spiders nest, in shadows under doors
Of rooms where centuries have died, and rest
In clouds along the blackening cracked floors
Of sties and closets, attics and wrecked tombs…
Thought's odour is so pale that in the air
Nostrils inhale, it disappears like fire

Put out by water. Drifting through the coils
Of the involved and sponge-like brain it frets
The fine-veined walls of secret mental cells,
Brushing their fragile fibre as with light
Nostalgic breezes: And it's then we sense
Remote presentiment of some intensely bright
Impending spiritual dawn, of which the pure
Immense illumination seems about to pour
In upon our existence from beyond
The edge of Knowing! But of that obscure
Deep presaging excitement shall remain
Briefly to linger in dry crannies of the brain
Not the least breath when fear-benumbed and frail
Our dying thought within the closely-sealed
Bone casket of the skull has flickered out,
And we've gone down into the odourless black soil.

A Tough Generation

To grow unguided at a time when none
Are sure where they should plant their sprig of trust;
When sunshine has no special mission to endow
With gold the rustic rose, which will run wild
And ramble from the garden to the wood
To train itself to climb the trunks of trees
If the old seedsman die and suburbs care
For sentimental cottage-flowers no more;
To grow up in a wood of rotted trees
In which it is not known which tree will be
First to disturb the silent sultry grove
With crack of doom, dead crackling and dread roar –
Will be infallibly to learn that first
One always owes a duty to oneself;
This much at least is certain: one must live.
And one may reach, without having to search
For much more lore than this, a shrewd maturity,
Equipped with adult aptitude to ape
All customary cant and current camouflage;
Nor be a whit too squeamish where the soul's concerned,

But hold out for the best black market price for it
Should need remind one that one has to live.
Yet just as sweetly, where no markets are,
An unkempt rose may for a season still
Trust its own beauty and disclose its heart
Even to the woodland shade, and as in sacrifice
Renounce its ragged petals one by one.

The Sacred Hearth

To George Barker

You must have been still sleeping, your wife there
Asleep beside you. All the old oak breathed: while slow,
How slow the intimate Spring night swelled through those depths
Of soundlessness and dew-chill shadow on towards the day.
Yet I, alone awake close by, was summoned suddenly
By distant voice more indistinct though more distinctly clear,
While all inaudible, than any dream's, calling on me to rise
And stumble barefoot down the stairs to seek the air
Outdoors, so sweet and somnolent, not cold, and at that hour
Suspending in its glass undrifting milk-strata of mist,
Stilled by the placid beaming of the adolescent moon.
There, blackly outlined in their moss-green light, they stood,
The trees of the small crabbed and weed-grown orchard,
Perfect as part of one of Calvert's idylls. It was then,
Wondering what calm magnet had thus drawn me from my bed,
I wandered out across the briar-bound garden, spellbound. Most
Mysterious and unrecapturable moment, when I stood
There staring back at the dark white nocturnal house,
And saw gleam through the lattices a light more pure than gold
Made sanguine with crushed roses, from the firelight that all night
Stayed flickering about the sacred hearth. As long as dawn
Hung fire behind the branch-hid sky, the strong
Magic of rustic slumber held unbroken; yet a song
Sprang wordless from inertia in my heart, to see how near
A neighbour strangeness ever stands to home. George, in the
                                                        wood
Of wandering among wood-hiding trees, where poets' art

Is how to whistle in the dark, where pockets all have holes,
All roofs for refugees have rents, we ought to know
That there can be for us no place quite alien and unknown,
No situation wholly hostile, if somewhere there burn
The faithful fire of vision still awaiting our return.

from *Miserere*

Ecce Homo

Whose is this horrifying face,
This putrid flesh, discoloured, flayed,
Fed on by flies, scorched by the sun?
Whose are these hollow red-filmed eyes
And thorn-spiked head and spear-stuck side?
Behold the Man: He is Man's Son.

Forget the legend, tear the decent veil
That cowardice or interest devised
To make their mortal enemy a friend,
To hide the bitter truth all His wounds tell,
Lest the great scandal be no more disguised:
He is in agony till the world's end,

And we must never sleep during that time!
He is suspended on the cross-tree now
And we are onlookers at the crime,
Callous contemporaries of the slow
Torture of God. Here is the hill
Made ghastly by His spattered blood

Whereon He hangs and suffers still:
See, the centurions wear riding-boots,
Black shirts and badges and peaked caps,
Greet one another with raised-arm salutes;
They have cold eyes, unsmiling lips;
Yet these His brothers know not what they do.

And on his either side hang dead
A labourer and a factory hand,
Or one is maybe a lynched Jew
And one a Negro or a Red,
Coolie or Ethiopian, Irishman,
Spaniard or German democrat.

Behind His lolling head the sky
Glares like a fiery cataract
Red with the murders of two thousand years
Committed in His name and by
Crusaders, Christian warriors
Defending faith and property.

Amid the plain beneath His transfixed hands,
Exuding darkness as indelible
As guilty stains, fanned by funereal
And lurid airs, besieged by drifting sands
And clefted landslides our about-to-be
Bombed and abandoned cities stand.

He who wept for Jerusalem
Now sees His prophecy extend
Across the greatest cities of the world,
A guilty panic reason cannot stem
Rising to raze them all as He foretold;
And He must watch this drama to the end.

Though often named, He is unknown
To the dark kingdoms at His feet
Where everything disparages His words,
And each man bears the common guilt alone
And goes blindfolded to his fate,
And fear and greed are sovereign lords.

The turning point of history
Must come. Yet the complacent and the proud
And who exploit and kill, may be denied –
Christ of Revolution and of Poetry –
The resurrection and the life
Wrought by your spirit's blood.

Involved in their own sophistry
The black priest and the upright man
Faced by subversive truth shall be struck dumb,
Christ of Revolution and of Poetry,
While the rejected and condemned become
Agents of the divine.

Not from a monstrance silver-wrought
But from the tree of human pain
Redeem our sterile misery,
Christ of Revolution and of Poetry,
That man's long journey through the night
May not have been in vain.

Prelude to a New Fin-de-Siècle

Incessant urging, curt, peremptory:
Write what you will, in verse or otherwise,
Intelligible, using simple metaphors.
Address a reader not just hypothetical
But flesh and blood in no need of harangues.
The time has come. We're on the very brink
Of what? Can any prophet, true or false,
Make himself heard above the mad uproar
Of all the mingling and ambiguous,
Self-righteous or dismayed denunciations,
Warnings and dire predictions that assail us from
All 'informed sources', media-debased and bent?

– If this is a poem, where are the images?
– What images suffice? Corpses and carrion,
Ubiquitous bloodshed, bigger, more beastly bombs,
Stockpiled atomic warheads, stanchless wounds,
Ruins and rubble, manic messiahs and mobs.
– But poets make beauty out of ghastliness…
– You think I want to? Think truth beautiful?
– 'A terrible beauty is born…' – It is indeed.

In youth I did in spite of everything
Believe with Keats and Shelley such things as
That poets can 'legislate' and prophesy;
Or like Stravinsky when he wrote 'The Rite'
Become transmitting vessels for new sounds
From an inspiring, unknown world within.
I'm over sixty now, my dubious gift has gone,
I can but grope for unexpected similes.

But now as in the 'Thirties I can once again
Feel passion and frustration and that sense
Of expectation, imminence and pressing need
To express something that just must be said.
Mature awareness knows that poetry
Today demands the essence and the minimum;
That only Silence such as God's could say the Whole.
One stark vocabulary at least remains.
The litany of lurid headline-names
Merely to mention which can nag the nerves:
Vietnam, Angola, Thailand and Pakistan,
Chile, Cambodia, Iran, Afghanistan,
Derry's Bogside, Belfast and Crossmaglen;
Up in Strathclyde or down on Porton Down,
On Three Mile Island or in Seveso Italy
Then there are Manson, Pol Pot and Amin,
To name at random just three myth-monsters,
Too many more to mention, all mass-murderers: –
None of them need an adjective and though we're sick
Of being sickened by them they will stay engraved
Or branded on even callous consciences.

And yet I yearn to end by trying to evoke
A summer dawn I saw when I was not yet eight,
And having risen early watched for an hour or more
A transcendental transformation of auroral clouds,
Like a prophetic vision granted from on high.
I cannot see much now. The dawn is always new
As nature is, however much we blind ourselves and try
To poison the Earth-Mother. But an ancient text
Tells of what I believe may happen soon today:
The raven disappears as night draws to its close,
Then as the day approaches the bird flies without wings;

It vomits forth the rainbow and its body becomes red,
And on its back a condensation of pure water forms.
For that which is above is still as that which is below
For the perfecting of the One Thing, which is now
As it shall ever be, World without End, D.V.

A Sarum Sestina

To Satish Kumar

Schooldays were centred round the tallest spire
In England, whose chime-pealing ruled our lives,
Spent in the confines of a leafy Close:
Chimes that controlled the hours we spent in singing,
Entered the classrooms to restrict our lessons
And punctuated the half-times of games.

The gravel courtyard where we played rough games
During the early break or after singing
In the Cathedral circled by the Close
And dominated by its soaring spire
Saw many minor dramas of our lives.
Such playgrounds predetermine later lessons.

Daily dividing services, meals, lessons,
Musical time resounded through the Close,
Metered existence like the rules of games.
What single cord connects most schoolboys' lives?
Not many consist first of stints of singing.
Our choral rearing paralleled a spire.

Reaching fourteen within sight of that spire
Unconsciously defined our growing lives,
As music's discipline informed our lessons.
We grew aware of how all round the Close
Households were run on lines that like our singing
Were regulated as communal games.

We sensed the serious need for fun and games,
What funny folk can populate a Close.
We relished festive meals as we did singing.
Beauty of buildings balanced boring lessons.
We looked relieved at times up at the spire
Balanced serene above parochial lives.

Grubby and trivial though our schoolboy lives
Were as all are, we found in singing
That liberation and delight result from lessons.
Under the ageless aegis of the spire
Seasonal feasts were ever-renewed games.
Box-hedges, limes and lawns line Sarum Close.

Choristers in that Close lead lucky lives.
They are taught by a spire and learn through singing
That hard lessons can be enjoyed like games.

Poems by

W.S. GRAHAM

Selected by

NESSIE DUNSMUIR

Nessie and Sydney Graham at the Gurnard's Head Hotel, 1959

Acknowledgement

Nessie Dunsmuir and Greville Press wish to thank Margaret and Michael Snow for their vital help in the production of the original pamphlet.

To ND

No two can meet the way that we have met,
Completely, like the marriage of fused stars
That streak their meteord lights each into each
And shuddering to the life of leaping light
Start down the sky charged to a double blaze.

No two can come the ways that we have come,
Like silver moonlight creeping over stones
On stream-banks, lighting every crystal vein
To Beauty's sadness. No, they have no dreams
To break the steady darkness of their night.

O Gentle Queen of the Afternoon

O gentle queen of the afternoon
Wave the last orient of tears.
No daylight comet ever breaks
On so sweet an archipelago
As love on love.

The fundamental negress built
In a cloudy descant of the stars
Surveys no sorrow, invents no limits
Till laughter the watcher of accident
Sways off to God.

O gentle queen of the afternoon
The dawn is rescued dead and risen.
Promise, O bush of blushing joy,
No daylight comet ever breaks
On so sweet an archipelago
As love on love.

Here Next the Chair I Was When Winter Went

Here next the chair I was when winter went
Down looking for distant bothies of love
And met birch-bright and by the blows of March
The farm bolder under and the din of burning.

I was what the whinfire works on towns
An orator from hill to kitchen dances.
In booths below bridges that spanned the crowds
Tinkers tricked glasses on lips and saw my eyes.

Like making a hut of fingers cupped for tears
Love burned my bush that was my burning mother.
The hoodiecrow in smoke in a wobbling wind
If a look is told for fortune saw my death.

So still going out in the morning of ash and air
My shovel swings. My tongue is a sick device.
Fear evening my boot says. The chair sees iceward
In the bitter hour so visible to death.

Shian Bay

Gulls set the long shore printed
With arrow steps over this morning's
Sands clean of a man's footprint
And set up question and reply
Over the serpentine jetty
And over the early coaches
Of foam noisily in rows
Driven in from the farout banks.

Last gale washed five into the bay's stretched arms,
Four drowned men and a boy drowned into shelter.
The stones roll out to shelter in the sea.

Gigha

That firewood pale with salt and burning green
Outfloats its men who waved with a sound of drowning
Their saltcut hands over mazes of this rough bay.

Quietly this morning beside the subsided herds
Of water I walk. The children wade the shallows.
The sun with long legs wades into the sea.

from *The Nightfishing*

4

Only leaned at rest
Where my home is cast
Cannonwise on silence
And the serving distance.

O my love, keep the day
Leaned at rest, leaned at rest.

Only breathed at ease
In that loneliness
Bragged into a voyage
On the maintaining image.

O my love, there we lay
Loved alone, loved alone.

Only graced in my
Changing madman who
Sings but has no time
To divine my room.

O my love, keep the day
Leaned at rest, leaned at rest.

What one place remains
Home as darkness quickens?

Letter VI

A day the wind was hardly
Shaking the youngest frond
Of April I went on
The high moor we know.
I put my childhood out
Into a cocked hat
And you moving the myrtle
Walked slowly over.
A sweet clearness became.
The Clyde sleeved in its firth
Reached and dazzled me.
I moved and caught the sweet
Courtesy of your mouth.
My breath to your breath.
And as you lay fondly
In the crushed smell of the moor
The courageous and just sun
Opened its door.
And there we lay halfway
Your body and my body
On the high moor. Without
A word then we went
Our ways. I heard the moor
Curling its cries far
Across the still loch.

The great verbs of the sea
Come down on us in a roar.
What shall I answer for?

I Leave This at Your Ear

For Nessie Dunsmuir

I leave this at your ear for when you wake,
A creature in its abstract cage asleep.
Your dreams blindfold you by the light they make.

The owl called from the naked-woman tree
As I came down by the Kyle farm to hear
Your house silent by the speaking sea.

I have come late but I have come before
Later with slaked steps from stone to stone
To hope to find you listening for the door.

I stand in the ticking room. My dear, I take
A moth kiss from your breath. The shore gulls cry.
I leave this at your ear for when you wake.

from *The Dark Dialogues*

4

Or I am always only
Thinking is this the time
To look elsewhere to turn
Towards what was it
I put myself out
Away from home to meet?
Was it this only? Surely
It is more than these words
See on my side
I went halfway to meet.

And there are other times.
But the times are always
Other and now what I meant
To say or hear or be
Lies hidden where exile
Too easily beckons.
What if the terrible times
Moving away find
Me in the end only
Staying where I am always
Unheard by a fault.

So to begin to return
At last neither early
Nor late and go my way
Somehow home across
This gesture become
Inhabited out of hand.
I stop and listen over
My shoulder and listen back
On language for that step
That seems to fall after
My own step in the dark.

Always must be the lost
Or where we turn, and all
For a sight of the dark again.
The farthest away, the least
To answer back come nearest.

And this place is taking
Its time from us though these
Two people or voices
Are not us nor has
The time they seem to move in
To do with what we think
Our own times are. Even
Where they are is only
This one inhuman place.
Yet somewhere a stone
Speaks and maybe a leaf
In the dark turns over.

And whoever I meant
To think I had met
Turns away further
Before me blinded by
This word and this word.

See how presently
The bull and the girl turn
From what they seemed to say,
And turn there above me
With that star-plotted head
Snorting on silence.
The legend turns. And on
Her starry face descried
Faintly astonishment.

The formal meadow fades
Over the ever-widening
Firth and in their time
That not unnatural pair
Turn slowly home.

This is no other place
Than where I am, between
This word and the next.
Maybe I should expect
To find myself only
Saying that again
Here now at the end.
Yet over the great
Gantries and cantilevers
Of love, a sky, real and
Particular is slowly
Startled into light.

O Why Am I So Bright

O why am I so bright
Flying in the night?

Why am I so fair
Flying through the air?

Will you let me in
After all I've done?

You are a good boy
On the fields of joy.

We see you as you go
Across the fields of snow.

We will not let you in.
Never. Never. Never.

A Walk To The Gulvas

1

Ness, shall we go for a walk?
I'll take you up to the Gulvas
You never really got to.

Put on your lovely yellow
Oilskin to meet the weather.

2

This bit of the road, Ness,
We know well, is different
Continually. Macadam
Has not smoothed it to death.
When the light keeks out, the road
Answers and shines up blue.
I thought we might have seen
Willie Wagtail from earlier.
Nessie, how many steps
Do we take from pole to pole
Going up this hill? I see
Your Blantyre rainy lashes.
The five wires are humming
Every good boy deserves
Favour. We have ascended
Into a mist. And this
Is where we swim the brambles
And catch the path across
The late or early moor
Between us and the Gulvas.

3

Hold on to me and step
Over the world's thorns.
We shall soon be on
The yellow and emerald moss
Of the Penwith moor.
Are you all right beside me?
What's your name and age
As though I did not know.
Are we getting older
At different speeds differently?

No, that's not it. The Gulvas
Cannot be seen from here.
Have we left it too late
Maybe the Gulvas is too
Far on a day like this
For us what are our ages
What are our foreign names
What are we doing here
Wet and scratched with the Gulvas
Moving away before us?

5

Let us go back. Reader,
You who have observed
Us at your price from word
To word through the rain,
Dont be put down. I'll come
Again and take you on
The great walk to the Gulvas.
Be well wrapped up against
The high moor and the brambles.

Loch Thom

1

Just for the sake of recovering
I walked backward from fifty-six
Quick years of age wanting to see,
And managed not to trip or stumble
To find Loch Thom and turned round
To see the stretch of my childhood
Before me. Here is the loch. The same
Long-beaked cry curls across
The heather-edges of the water held

Between the hills a boyhood's walk
Up from Greenock. It is the morning.

And I am here with my mammy's
Bramble jam scones in my pocket.
The Firth is miles and I have come
Back to find Loch Thom maybe
In this light does not recognise me.

This is a lonely freshwater loch.
No farms on the edge. Only
Heather grouse-moor stretching
Down to Greenock and One Hope
Street or stretching away across
Into the blue moors of Ayrshire.

2

And almost I am back again
Wading the heather down to the edge
To sit. The minnows go by in shoals
Like iron-filings in the shallows.
My mother is dead. My father is dead
And all the trout I used to know
Leaping from their sad rings are dead.

3

I drop my crumbs into the shallow
Weed for the minnows and pinheads.
You see that I will have to rise
And turn round and get back where
My running age will slow for a moment
To let me on. It is a colder
Stretch of water than I remember.

The curlew's cry travelling still
Kills me fairly. In front of me
The grouse flurry and settle. GOBACK
GOBACK GOBACK FAREWELL LOCH THOM.

from *Implements in Their Places*

73

Of air he knows nor does he speak
To earth. The day is sailing round
His heavenly wings. Daisies and cups
Of butter and dragonflies stop
Their meadow life to look up wondering
How out of what ridiculous season
The wingèd one descends.

74

Somewhere our belonging particles
Believe in us. If we could only find them.

To My Wife at Midnight

1

Are you to say goodnight
And turn away under
The blanket of your delight?

Are you to let me go
Alone to sleep beside you
Into the drifting snow?

Where we each reach,
Sleeping alone together,
Nobody can touch.

Is the cat's window open?
Shall I turn into your back?
And what is to happen?

What is to happen to us
And what is to happen to each
Of us asleep in our places?

2

I mean us both going
Into sleep at our ages
To sleep and get our fairing.

They have all gone home.
Night beasts are coming out.
The black wood of Madron

Is just waking up.
I hear the rain outside
To help me to go to sleep.

Nessie, dont let my soul
Skip and miss a beat
And cause me to fall.

3

Are you asleep I say
Into the back of your neck
For you not to hear me.

Are you asleep? I hear
Your heart under the pillow
Saying my dear my dear

My dear for all it's worth.
Where is the dun's moor
Which began your breath?

4

Ness, to tell you the truth
I am drifting away
Down to fish for the saithe.

Is the cat's window open?
The weather is on my shoulder
And I am drifting down

Into O can you hear me
Among your Dunsmuir Clan?
Are you coming out to play?

5

Did I behave badly
On the field at Culloden?
I lie sore-wounded now

By all activities, and
The terrible acts of my time
Are only a distant sound.

With responsibility
I am drifting off
Breathing regularly

Into my younger days
To play the games of Greenock
Beside the sugar-house quays.

6

Nessie Dunsmuir, I say
Wheesht wheesht to myself
To help me now to go

Under into somewhere
In the redcoat rain.
Buckle me for the war.

Are you to say goodnight
And kiss me and fasten
My drowsy armour tight?

My dear camp-follower,
Hap the blanket round me
And tuck in a flower.

Maybe from my sleep
In the stoure at Culloden
I'll see you here asleep

In your lonely place.

'Yesterday Only'
and other poems

Poems by
ROBERT GRAVES

Selected by
BERYL GRAVES

Robert and Beryl Graves, Deià, Majorca, *c.* 1950

FOREWORD

In selecting these poems I have been only too aware of the first line of Graves's poem *Whole Love*: 'Every choice is always the wrong choice'. As it is impossible to choose thirty-two poems out of 1,202, especially with so many pleading to be included, I must offer this selection as yet another 'wrong choice', but one at least which includes many of my favourites.

2000   BERYL GRAVES

Two Fusiliers

And have we done with War at last?
Well, we've been lucky devils both,
And there's no need of pledge or oath
To bind our lovely friendship fast,
By firmer stuff
Close bound enough.

By wire and wood and stake we're bound,
By Fricourt and by Festubert,
By whipping rain, by the sun's glare,
By all the misery and loud sound,
By a Spring day,
By Picard clay.

Show me the two so closely bound
As we, by the wet bond of blood,
By friendship blossoming from mud,
By Death: we faced him, and we found
Beauty in Death,
In dead men, breath.

1917

I Am the Star of Morning

I am the Star of Morning poised between
The dead night and the coming of the sun,
Yet neither relic of the dark nor pointing
The angry day to come. My virtue is
My own, a mild light, an enduring courage;
And the remembering ancient tribe of birds
Sing blithest at my showing; only Man
Sleeps on and stirs rebellious in his sleep.
Lucifer, Lucifer, am I, millstone-crushed
Between conflicting powers of doubleness,
By envious Night lost in her myriad more

Counterfeit glints, in day-time quite overwhelmed
By tyrant blazing of the warrior sun.
Yet some, my prophets who at midnight held me
Fixedly framed in their observant glass,
By daylight also, sinking well-shafts deep
For water and for coolness of pure thought,
Gaze up and far above them see me shining,
Me, single natured, without gender, one,
The only spark of Godhead unresolved.

1923

Full Moon

As I walked out that sultry night,
 I heard the stroke of One.
The moon, attained to her full height,
 Stood beaming like the sun:
She exorcized the ghostly wheat
To mute assent in love's defeat,
 Whose tryst had now begun.

The fields lay sick beneath my tread,
 A tedious owlet cried,
A nightingale above my head
 With this or that replied –
Like man and wife who nightly keep
Inconsequent debate in sleep
 As they dream side by side.

Your phantom wore the moon's cold mask,
 My phantom wore the same;
Forgetful of the feverish task
 In hope of which they came,
Each image held the other's eyes
And watched a grey distraction rise
 To cloud the eager flame –

To cloud the eager flame of love,
    To fog the shining gate;
They held the tyrannous queen above
    Sole mover of their fate,
They glared as marble statues glare
Across the tessellated stair
    Or down the halls of state.

And now warm earth was Arctic sea,
    Each breath came dagger-keen;
Two bergs of glinting ice were we,
    The broad moon sailed between;
There swam the mermaids, tailed and finned,
And love went by upon the wind
    As though it had not been.

1923

The North Window

When the chapel is lit and sonorous with ploughmen's praise,
When matron and child crouch low to the Lord of Days,
When the windows are shields of greyness all about,
For the glowing lamps within and the storm without;
On this Eve of All Souls (suicides too have souls)
The damned to the Northward rise from their tablets and scrolls,
With infants unbaptized that lie without ease,
With women betrayed, their mothers, who murdered these,
They make them a furious chapel of wind and gloom
With, Southward, one stained window *The Hour of Doom*
Lit up by the lamp of the righteous beaming through
With the scene reversed, and the legend backwards too,
Displaying in scarlet and gold the Creator who damns
Who has thrust on His Left the bleating sheep and the lambs,
Who has fixed on His Right the goats and kids accursed,
With *Omega: Alpha* restoring the last as first:
Then the psalms to God that issue hence or thence
Ring blasphemy each to the other's Omnipotence.

1924

A History

The Palmist said: 'In your left hand, which shews your inheritance,
the Line of Head dips steeply towards Luna. In your right hand,
which shews your development, there is a determined effort to
escape into less melancholy thinking.' I said nothing, but shewed
him this sonnet: –

When in my first and loneliest love I saw
    The sun swim down in tears to meet the sea,
When woods and clouds and mountains massed their awe
    To whelm the house of torment that was me,
When spirits below the cromlech heard me pass
    Belling their hate with such malignant cries
That horror and anguish rustled through the grass
    And the very flowers glared up with oafish eyes,

Then round I turned where rose the death-white Fay
    And knew her well that exercised her wand,
That spurred my heart with rowellings day by day
    To the very reach of madness and beyond,
Thee, Moon, whom now I flout, by thought made bold.
    Naked, my Joseph's garment in thy hold.

1924

The Presence

Why say 'death'? Death is neither harsh nor kind:
Other pleasures or pains could hold the mind
If she were dead. For dead is gone indeed,
Lost beyond recovery and need,
Discarded, ended, rotted underground –
Of whom no personal feature could be found
To stand out from the soft blur evenly spread
On memory, if she were truly dead.

But living still, barred from accustomed use
Of body and dress and motion, with profuse
Reproaches (since this anguish of her grew
Do I still love her as I swear I do?)
She fills the house and garden terribly
With her bewilderment, accusing me,
Till every stone and flower, table and book,
Cries out her name, pierces me with her look,
'You are deaf, listen!
You are blind, see!'
                How deaf or blind,
When horror of the grave maddens the mind
With those same pangs that lately choked her breath,
Altered her substance, and made sport of death?

1925

From an Upper Window

Dark knoll, where distant furrows end
In rocks beyond the river-bend,
    I make my visionary stand
    In your secure well-wooded land
Where idle paths of idle fancy tend.

The charts that threaten all things free
With bondage of geography
    That loop you with a road way round
    Or pin you to some parish bound
Cannot withdraw your loveliness from me.

Nor though I went with hound and stick
With compass and arithmetic
    To gain myself a closer view
    Could I in space come up with you
Your glades with moving shades and colours quick.

You are remote in space and time
As inenarrable in rhyme,
  Yet by this very rareness doubt
  That you are you is blotted out –
Hill of green hopes with slopes no foot may climb.

c. 1925

Return Fare

And so to Ireland on an Easter Tuesday
To a particular place I could not find.
A sleeping man beside me in the boat-train
Sat whistling *Liliburlero* in his sleep;
Not, I had thought, a possible thing, yet so.
And through a port-hole of the Fishguard boat,
That was the hospital-boat of twelve years back,
Passengered as before with doubt and dying,
I saw the moon through glass, but a waning moon,
Bad luck, self-doubtful, so once more I slept.
And then the engines woke me up by stopping.
The piers of the quay loomed up. So I went up.
The sun shone rainily and jokingly,
And everyone joked at his own expense,
And the priest declared 'nothing but fishing tackle,'
Laughing provokingly. I could not laugh.
And the hard cackling laughter of the men
And the false whinnying laughter of the girls
Grieved me. The telegraph-clerk said, grieving too,
'St. Peter, he's two words in the Free State now,
So that's a salmon due.' I paid the fish.
And everyone I asked about the place
Knew the place well, but not its whereabouts,
And the black-shawled peasant woman asked me then,
Wasn't I jaded? And she grieved to me
Of the apple and the expulsion from the garden.
Ireland went by, and went by as I saw her
When last I saw her for the first time
Exactly how I had seen her all the time.

And I found the place near Sligo, not the place,
So back to England on the Easter Thursday.

1929

Saint

This Blatant Beast was finally overcome
And in no secret tourney: wit and fashion
Flocked out and for compassion
Wept as the Red Cross Knight pushed the blade home.

The people danced and sang the paeans due,
Roasting whole oxen on the public spit;
Twelve mountain peaks were lit
With bonfires; yet their hearts were doubt and rue.

Therefore no grave was deep enough to hold
The Beast, who after days came thrusting out,
Wormy from rump to snout,
His yellow cere-cloth patched with the grave's mould.

Nor could sea hold him: anchored with huge rocks,
He swelled and buoyed them up, paddling ashore
As evident as before
With deep-sea ooze and salty creaking bones.

Lime could not burn him, nor the sulphur fire:
So often as the good Knight bound him there,
With stink of singeing hair
And scorching flesh the corpse rolled from the pyre.

In the city-gutter would the Beast lie
Praising the Knight for all his valorous deeds:
'Ay, on those water-meads
He slew even me. These death-wounds testify.'

The Knight governed that city, a man shamed
And shrunken: for the Beast was over-dead,
With wounds no longer red
But gangrenous and loathsome and inflamed.

Not all the righteous judgements he could utter,
Nor mild laws frame, nor public works repair,
Nor wars wage, in despair,
Could bury that same Beast, crouched in the gutter.

A fresh remembrance-banquet to forestall,
The Knight turned hermit, went without farewell
To a far mountain-cell;
But the Beast followed as his seneschal,

And there drew water for him and hewed wood
With vacant howling laughter; else all day
Noisome with long decay
Sunning himself at the cave's entry stood.

Would bawl to pilgrims for a dole of bread
To feed the sick saint who once vanquished him
With spear so stark and grim;
Would set a pillow of grass beneath his head,
Would fetch him fever-wort from the pool's brim –
And crept into his grave when he was dead.

1930

The Felloe'd Year

The pleasure of summer was its calm success
Over winter past and winter sequent:
The pleasure of winter was a warm counting,
'Summer comes again, when, surely.'
This pleasure and that pleasure touched
In a perpetual spring-with-autumn ache,
A creak and groan of season,
In which all moved,
In which all move yet – I the same, yet praying
That the twelve spokes of this round-felloe'd year
Be a fixed compass, not a turning wheel.

                                                              1931

Recalling War

Entrance and exit wounds are silvered clean,
The track aches only when the rain reminds.
The one-legged man forgets his leg of wood,
The one-armed man his jointed wooden arm.
The blinded man sees with his ears and hands
As much or more than once with both his eyes.
Their war was fought these twenty years ago
And now assumes the nature-look of time,
As when the morning traveller turns and views
His wild night-stumbling carved into a hill.

What, then, was war? No mere discord of flags
But an infection of the common sky
That sagged ominously upon the earth
Even when the season was the airiest May.
Down pressed the sky and we, oppressed, thrust out
Boastful tongue, clenched fist and valiant yard.
Natural infirmities were out of mode,
For Death was young again: patron alone
Of healthy dying, premature fate-spasm.

Fear made fine bed-fellows. Sick with delight
At life's discovered transitoriness,
Our youth became all-flesh and waived the mind.
Never was such antiqueness of romance,
Such tasty honey oozing from the heart.
And old importances came swimming back –
Wine, meat, log-fires, a roof over the head,
A weapon at the thigh, surgeons at call.
Even there was a use again for God –
A word of rage in lack of meat, wine, fire,
In ache of wounds beyond all surgeoning.

War was return of earth to ugly earth,
War was foundering of sublimities,
Extinction of each happy art and faith
By which the world had still kept head in air,
Protesting logic or protesting love,
Until the unendurable moment struck –
The inward scream, the duty to run mad.

And we recall the merry ways of guns –
Nibbling the walls of factory and church
Like a child, piecrust; felling groves of trees
Like a child, dandelions with a switch.
Machine-guns rattle toy-like from a hill,
Down in a row the brave tin-soldiers fall:
A sight to be recalled in elder days
When learnedly the future we devote
To yet more boastful visions of despair.

1935

A Love Story

The full moon easterly rising, furious,
Against a winter sky ragged with red;
The hedges high in snow, and owls raving –
Solemnities not easy to withstand:
A shiver wakes the spine.

In boyhood, having encountered the scene,
I suffered horror: I fetched the moon home,
With owls and snow, to nurse in my head
Throughout the trials of a new Spring,
Famine unassuaged.

But fell in love, and made a lodgement
Of love on those chill ramparts.
Her image was my ensign: snows melted,
Hedges sprouted, the moon tenderly shone,
The owls trilled with tongues of nightingale.

These were all lies, though they matched the time,
And brought me less than luck: her image
Warped in the weather, turned beldamish.
Then back came winter on me at a bound,
The pallid sky heaved with a moon-quake.

Dangerous it had been with love-notes
To serenade Queen Famine.
In tears I recomposed the former scene,
Let the snow lie, watched the moon rise, suffered the owls,
Paid homage to them of unevent.

                                                    1939

Despite and Still

Have you not read
The words in my head,
And I made part
Of your own heart?
We have been such as draw
The losing straw –
You of your gentleness,
I of my rashness,
Both of despair –
Yet still might share
This happy will:
To love despite and still.
Never let us deny
The thing's necessity,
But, O, refuse
To choose
Where chance may seem to give
Loves in alternative.

1941

Theseus and Ariadne

High on his figured couch beyond the waves
He dreams, in dream recalling her set walk
Down paths of oyster-shell bordered with flowers,
Across the shadowy turf below the vines.
He sighs: 'Deep sunk in my erroneous past
She haunts the ruins and the ravaged lawns.'

Yet still unharmed it stands, the regal house
Crooked with age and overtopped by pines
Where first he wearied of her constancy.
And with a surer foot she goes than when
Dread of his hate was thunder in the air,
When the pines agonized with flaws of wind

And flowers glared up at her with frantic eyes.
Of him, now all is done, she never dreams
But calls a living blessing down upon
What he supposes rubble and rank grass;
Playing the queen to nobler company.

1941

To Juan at the Winter Solstice

There is one story and one story only
That will prove worth your telling,
Whether as learned bard or gifted child;
To it all lines or lesser gauds belong
That startle with their shining
Such common stories as they stray into.

Is it of trees you tell, their months and virtues,
Of strange beasts that beset you,
Of birds that croak at you the Triple will?
Or of the Zodiac and how slow it turns
Below the Boreal Crown,
Prison of all true kings that ever reigned?

Water to water, ark again to ark,
From woman back to woman:
So each new victim treads unfalteringly
The never altered circuit of his fate,
Bringing twelve peers as witness
Both to his starry rise and starry fall.

Or is it of the Virgin's silver beauty,
All fish below the thighs?
She in her left hand bears a leafy quince;
When with her right she crooks a finger, smiling,
How may the King hold back?
Royally then he barters life for love.

Or of the undying snake from chaos hatched,
Whose coils contain the ocean,
Into whose chops with naked sword he springs,
Then in black water, tangled by the reeds,
Battles three days and nights,
To be spewed up beside her scalloped shore?

Much snow is falling, winds roar hollowly,
The owl hoots from the elder,
Fear in your heart cries to the loving-cup:
Sorrow to sorrow as the sparks fly upward.
The log groans and confesses:
There is one story and one story only.

Dwell on her graciousness, dwell on her smiling,
Do not forget what flowers
The great boar trampled down in ivy time.
Her brow was creamy as the crested wave,
Her sea-grey eyes were wild
But nothing promised that is not performed.

1945

Nuns and Fish

Circling the circlings of their fish
    Nuns walk in white and pray;
    For he is chaste as they,
    Who was dark-faced and hot in Silvia's day,
And in his pool drowns each unspoken wish.

1946

The Last Day of Leave (1916)

We five looked out over the moor
At rough hills blurred with haze, and a still sea:
Our tragic day, bountiful from the first.

We would spend it by the lily lake
(High in a fold beyond the farthest ridge),
Following the cart-track till it faded out.

The time of berries and bell-heather;
Yet all that morning nobody went by
But shepherds and one old man carting turfs.

We were in love: he with her, she with him,
And I, the youngest one, the odd man out,
As deep in love with a yet nameless muse.

No cloud; larks and heath-butterflies,
And herons undisturbed fishing the streams;
A slow cool breeze that hardly stirred the grass.

When we hurried down the rocky slope,
A flock of ewes galloping off in terror,
There shone the waterlilies, yellow and white.

Deep water and a shelving bank.
Off went our clothes and in we went, all five,
Diving like trout between the lily groves.

The basket had been nobly filled:
Wine and fresh rolls, chicken and pineapple –
Our braggadocio under threat of war.

The fire on which we boiled our kettle
We fed with ling and rotten blackthorn root;
And the coffee tasted memorably of peat.

Two of us might stray off together
But never less than three kept by the fire,
Focus of our uncertain destinies.

We spoke little, our minds in tune –
A sigh or laugh would settle any theme;
The sun so hot it made the rocks quiver.

But when it rolled down level with us,
Four pairs of eyes sought mine as if appealing
For a blind-fate-aversive afterword: –

'Do you remember the lily lake?
We were all there, all five of us in love,
Not one yet killed, widowed or broken-hearted.'

1947

Counting the Beats

You, love, and I,
(He whispers) you and I,
And if no more than only you and I
What care you or I?

Counting the beats,
Counting the slow heart beats,
The bleeding to death of time in slow heart beats,
Wakeful they lie.

Cloudless day,
Night, and a cloudless day,
Yet the huge storm will burst upon their heads one day
From a bitter sky.

Where shall we be,
(She whispers) where shall we be,
When death strikes home, O where then shall we be
Who were you and I?

Not there but here,
(He whispers) only here,
As we are, here, together, now and here,
Always you and I.

Counting the beats,
Counting the slow heart beats,
The bleeding to death of time in slow heart beats,
Wakeful they lie.

1951

The Devil at Berry Pomeroy

Snow and fog unseasonable,
The cold remarkable,
Children sickly;
Green fruit lay thickly
Under the crab-tree
And the wild cherry.
I heard witches call
Their imps to the Hall:
'Hey, Ilemauzar,
Sack-and-Sugar,
Peck-in-the-Crown,
Come down, come down!'
I heard bells toll
For a monster's soul
That was born, half dead,
With a double head;
I saw ghosts leap
From the ruined keep;
I saw blows thwack
On the raw back
Of a dying ass.
Blight was on the grass,
Poison in the cup
(Lover, drink up!),
With envy, slander,

Weasels a-wander,
Incest done
Between mother and son,
Murder of hags
For their money-bags,
Wrath, rape,
And the shadowy ape
Which a lady, weeping,
Leads by a string
From first twilight
Until past midnight
Through the Castle yard –
'Blow winds, blow hard!'
So the Devil snaps his chain
And renews his reign
To the little joy
Of Berry Pomeroy.

1953

Dialogue on the Headland

SHE: You'll not forget these rocks and what I told you?
HE: How could I? Never: whatever happens.
SHE: What do you think might happen?
    Might you fall out of love? – did you mean that?
HE: Never, never! 'Whatever' was a sop
    For jealous listeners in the shadows.
SHE: You haven't answered me. I asked:
    'What do you think might happen?'
HE: Whatever happens: though the skies should fall
    Raining their larks and vultures in our laps –
SHE: 'Though the seas turn to slime' – say that –
    'Though water-snakes be hatched with six heads.'
HE: Though the seas turn to slime, or tower
    In an arching wave above us, three miles high –
SHE: 'Though she should break with you' – dare you say that?
    'Though she deny her words on oath.'
HE: I had that in my mind to say, or nearly;

	It hurt so much I choked it back.
SHE:	How many other days can't you forget?
	How many other loves and landscapes?
HE:	You are jealous?
SHE:	Damnably.
HE:	The past is past.
SHE:	And this?
HE:	Whatever happens, this goes on.
SHE:	Without a future? Sweetheart, tell me now:
	What do you want of me? I must know that.
HE:	Nothing that isn't freely mine already.
SHE:	Say what is freely yours and you shall have it.
HE:	Nothing that, loving you, I could dare take.
SHE:	O, for an answer with no 'nothing' in it!
HE:	Then give me everything that's left.
SHE:	Left after what?
HE:	After whatever happens:
	Skies have already fallen, seas are slime,
	Watersnakes poke and peer six-headedly –
SHE:	And I lie snugly in the Devil's arms.
HE:	I said: 'Whatever happens.' Are you crying?
SHE:	You'll not forget me – ever, ever, ever?

1953

Ouzo Unclouded

Here is ouzo (she said) to try you:
Better not drowned in water,
Better not chilled with ice,
Not sipped at thoughtfully,
Nor toped in secret.
Drink it down (she said) unclouded
At a blow, this tall glass full,
But keep your eyes on mine
Like a true Arcadian acorn-eater.

1961

The Hearth

Here it begins: the worm of love breeding
Among red embers of a hearth-fire
Turns to a chick, is slowly fledged,
And will hop from lap to lap in a ring
Of eager children basking at the blaze.

But the luckless man who never sat there,
Nor borrowed live coals from the sacred source
To warm a hearth of his own making,
Nor bedded lay under pearl-grey wings
In dutiful content,

How shall he watch at the stroke of midnight
Dove become phoenix, plumed with green and gold?
Or be caught up by jewelled talons
And haled away to a fastness of the hills
Where an unveiled woman, black as Mother Night,
Teaches him a new degree of love
And the tongues and songs of birds?

1964

The Narrow Sea

With you for mast and sail and flag,
And anchor never known to drag,
Death's narrow but oppressive sea
Looks not unnavigable to me.

1968

Song: *Fig Tree in Leaf*

One day in early Spring
Upon bare branches perching
    Great companies of birds are seen
    Clad all at once in pilgrim green
Their news of love to bring:

Their fig tree parable,
For which the world is watchful,
    Retold with shining wings displayed:
    Her secret flower, her milk, her shade,
Her scarlet, blue and purple.

1968

What We Did Next

What we did next, neither of us remembers....
Still, the key turned, the wide bronze gate creaked open
And there before us in profuse detail
Spread Paradise: its lawns dappled with petals,
Pomegranate trees in quincunx, corn in stooks;
Plantations loud with birds, pools live with fish,
And unborn children blue as bonfire-smoke
Crouching entranced to see the grand serpent
Writhe in and out of long rock-corridors,
Rattling his coils of gold –
Or the jewelled toad from whose immense mouth
Burst out the four great rivers.... To be there
Was always to be there, without grief, always,
Superior to all chance, or change, or death....

What we did next, neither of us remembers.

1969

Song: *Yesterday Only*

Not today, not tomorrow,
Yesterday only:
A long-lasting yesterday
Devised by us to swallow
Today with tomorrow.

When was your poem hidden
Underneath my pillow,
When was your rose-bush planted
Underneath my window –
Yesterday only?

Green leaves, red roses,
Blazoned upon snow,
A long-lasting yesterday,
Today with tomorrow,
Always and only.

1969

Song: *Olive Tree*

Call down a blessing
On that green sapling,
A sudden blessing
For true love's sake
On that green sapling
Framed by our window
With her leaves twinkling
As we lie awake.
Two birds flew from her
In the eye of morning
Their folded feathers
In the sun to shake.

Augury recorded,
Vision rewarded
With an arrow flying
With a sudden sting,
With a sure blessing,
With a double dart,
With a starry ring,
With music from the mountains
In the air, in the heart
This bright May morning
Re-echoing.

1969

A Dream of Frances Speedwell

I fell in love at my first evening party.
You were tall and fair, just seventeen perhaps,
Talking to my two sisters. I kept silent
And never since have loved a tall fair girl,
Until last night in the small windy hours
When, floating up an unfamiliar staircase
And into someone's bedroom, there I found her
Posted beside the window in half-light
Wearing that same white dress with lacy sleeves.
She beckoned. I came closer. We embraced
Inseparably until the dream faded.
Her eyes shone clear and blue....

Who was it, though, impersonated you?

1972

The Moon's Last Quarter

So daylight dies.
The moon's in full decline,
Nor can those misted early stars outshine her.
But what of love, counted on to discount
Recurrent terror of the moon's last quarter?

Child, take my hand, kiss it finger by finger!
Can true love fade? I do not fear death
But only pity, with forgetfulness
Of love's timeless vocabulary

And an end to poetry
With death's mad aircraft rocketing from the sky.
Child, take my hand!

1973

The Green Woods of Unrest

Let the weeks end as well they must
Not with clouds of scattered dust
But in pure certainty of sun –
And with gentle winds outrun
By the love that we contest
In these green woods of unrest.
You, love, are beauty's self indeed,
Never the harsh pride of need.

1974

At the Gate

Where are poems? Why do I now write none?
This can mean no lack of pens, nor lack of love,
But need perhaps of an increased magic –
Where have my ancient powers suddenly gone?

Tonight I caught a glimpse of her at the gate
Grappling a monster never found before,
And jerking back its head. Had I come too late?
Her eyes blazed fire and I could look no more.

What could she hold against me? Never yet
Had I lied to her or thwarted her desire,
Rejecting prayers that I could never forget,
Stealing green leaves to light an alien fire.

1974

The Unpenned Poem

Should I wander with no frown, these idle days,
My dark hair trespassing on its pale brow –
If so, without companionship or praise,
Must I revisit marshes where frogs croak
Like me, mimicking penitential ways?

Are you still anchored to my slow, warm heart
After long years of drawing nightly nearer
And visiting our haunted room, timely
Ruffling its corners with love's hidden mop?
And still must we not part?

What is a poem if as yet unpenned
Though truthful and emancipated still
From what may never yet appear,
From the flowery riches of still silent song
From golden hours of a wakeful Spring?

Approach me, Rhyme; advise me, Reason!
The wind blows gently from the mountain top.
Let me display three penetrative wounds
White and smooth in this wrinkled skin of mine,
Still unacknowledged by the flesh beneath.

A poem may be trapped here suddenly,
Thrusting its adder's head among the leaves,
Without reason or rhyme, dumb –
Or if not dumb, then with a single voice
Robbed of its chorus.

Here looms November. When last did I approach
Paper with ink, pen, and the half truth?
Advise me, Reason!

1975

Poems by

HAROLD PINTER

Selected by

ANTONIA FRASER

Harold Pinter and Antonia Fraser after their wedding,
27 November 1980

FOREWORD

I was introduced to Harold's poetry shortly after we first met in January 1975. He wrote a poem called 'Paris' which celebrated our first jaunt together in May that year, and poetry has remained central to our shared life ever since.

All the poems I have chosen – with one exception – were written in the years following our first meeting, four of them directly to me. Apart from 'Paris', these are 'I Know the Place', 'Denmark Hill' and 'It is Here – for A'. (Are you the A in question?, asked my mother, cautious where poetry is concerned.) The one exception to this rule, 'Later', belongs to the summer of 1974, and Harold tells me that it expresses his mood at that time, so I have included it as a picture frame.

Harold is fortunate, I believe, to be able to mark the turning-points in his life through poetry, not only 'Paris' but 'Ghost' after the death of his first wife and 'Death' written just after the registration of his father's death at Hove Town Hall. 'Cancer Cells', the last poem in the book chronologically, refers to his recent illness.

So poetry remains central to his life, and to ours. Recently at dinner in a local restaurant Harold suggested lightly that death might be necessary otherwise the planet would be fatally overloaded. I responded with a sort-of-haiku written on a napkin:

> If there was no death
> In all the crowds
> How would I have met you?

This was Harold's answer:

> You'd find me turning from the long bar
> Glasses raised,
> One for you, one for me.

21 *April* 2002   ANTONIA FRASER

For Edna O'Brien
our friend

Paris

The curtain white in folds,
She walks two steps and turns,
The curtain still, the light
Staggers in her eyes.

The lamps are golden.
Afternoon leans, silently.
She dances in my life.
The white day burns.

1975

Later

Later. I look out at the moon.
I lived here once.
I remember the song.

Later. No sound here.
Moon on linoleum.
A child frowning.

Later. A voice singing.
I open the back door.
I lived here once.

Later. I open the back door
Light gone. Dead trees.
Dead linoleum. Later.

Later. Blackness moving very fast.
Blackness fatly.
I live here now.

1974

I know the place

I know the place.
It is true.
Everything we do
Corrects the space
Between death and me
And you.

1975

Message

Jill. Fred phoned. He can't make tonight.
He said he'd call again, as soon as poss.
I said (on your behalf) OK, no sweat.
He said to tell you he was fine,
Only the crap, he said, you know, it sticks,
The crap you have to fight.
You're sometimes nothing but a walking shithouse.

I was well acquainted with the pong myself,
I told him, and I counselled calm.
Don't let the fuckers get you down,
Take the lid off the kettle a couple of minutes,
Go on the town, burn someone to death,
Find another tart, give her some hammer,
Live while you're young, until it palls,
Kick the first blind man you meet in the balls.

Anyway he'll call again.

I'll be back in time for tea.

Your loving mother.

1977

Denmark Hill

Well, at least you're there,
And when I come into the room,
You'll stand, your hands linked,
And smile,
Or, if asleep,
Wake.

1977

Joseph Brearley 1909–1977
(Teacher of English)

Dear Joe, I'd like to walk with you
From Clapton Pond to Stamford Hill
And on,
Through Manor House to Finsbury Park,
And back,
On the dead 653 trolleybus,
To Clapton Pond,
And walk across the shadows on to Hackney Downs,
And stop by the old bandstand,
You tall in moonlight,
And the quickness in which it all happened,
And the quick shadow in which it persists.

You're gone. I'm at your side,
Walking with you from Clapton Pond to Finsbury Park,
And on, and on.

1977

Poem

The lights glow.
What will happen next?

Night has fallen.
The rain stops.
What will happen next?

Night will deepen.
He does not know
What I will say to him.

When he has gone
I'll have a word in his ear
And say what I was about to say
At the meeting about to happen
Which has now taken place.

But he said nothing
At the meeting about to take place.
It is only now that he turns and smiles
And whispers:
'I do not know
What will happen next.'

1981

Ghost

I felt soft fingers at my throat
It seemed someone was strangling me

The lips were hard as they were sweet
It seemed someone was kissing me

My vital bones about to crack
I gaped into another's eyes

I saw it was a face I knew
A face as sweet as it was grim

It did not smile it did not weep
Its eyes were wide and white its skin

I did not smile I did not weep
I raised my hand and touched its cheek

1983

Before They Fall

Before they fall
The obese stars
Dumb stones dumb lumps of light

Before they gasp before they

Before they gasp
And spit out their last blood

Before they drop before they

Before they drop
In spikes of frozen fire

Before they choke before they

Before they choke
In a last heartburn of stunk light

Let me say this

1983

Cricket at Night

They are still playing cricket at night
They are playing the game in the dark
They're on guard for a backlash of light

They are losing the ball at long leg
They are trying to learn how the dark
Helps the yorker knock back the off-peg

They are trying to find a new trick
Where the ball moves to darkness from light
They're determined to paint the scene black
But a blackness compounded by white
They are dying to pass a new law
Where blindness is deemed to be sight

They are still playing cricket at night

1995

Death

Births and Deaths Registration Act 1953

Where was the dead body found?
Who found the dead body?
Was the dead body dead when found?
How was the dead body found?

Who was the dead body?

Who was the father or daughter or brother
Or uncle or sister or mother or son
Of the dead and abandoned body?

Was the body dead when abandoned?
Was the body abandoned?
By whom had it been abandoned?

Was the dead body naked or dressed for a journey?

What made you declare the dead body dead?
Did you declare the dead body dead?
How well did you know the dead body?
How did you know the dead body was dead?

Did you wash the dead body
Did you close both its eyes
Did you bury the body
Did you leave it abandoned
Did you kiss the dead body

1997

Cancer Cells

'Cancer cells are those which have forgotten how to die'
Nurse, Royal Marsden hospital

They have forgotten how to die
And so extend their killing life.

I and my tumour dearly fight.
Let's hope a double death is out.

I need to see my tumour dead
A tumour which forgets to die
But plans to murder me instead.

But I remember how to die
Though all my witnesses are dead.
But I remember what they said
Of tumours which would render them
As blind and dumb as they had been
Before the birth of that disease
Which brought the tumour into play.

The black cells will dry up and die
Or sing with joy and have their way.
They breed so quietly night and day,
You never know, they never say.

2002

It Is Here

For A

What sound was that?

I turn away, into the shaking room.

What was that sound that came in on the dark?
What is this maze of light it leaves us in?
What is this stance we take,
To turn away and then turn back?
What did we hear?

It was the breath we took when we first met.

Listen. It is here.

1990

Poems by

ANNE RIDLER

Selected by

VIVIAN RIDLER

Anne and Vivian Ridler, Oxford, 1994

FOREWORD

Anne Ridler's first book of poems was published by the Oxford University Press in 1939, the year after our marriage. It was printed by me at the Bunhill Press (a small plant started by Theodore Besterman, the wealthy bibliographer) in Bunhill Row, over-looking Bunhill Fields where William Blake and John Bunyan lie buried.

In the autumn of 1940 the Press was completely destroyed in one of the heaviest bombing raids of the war, when the fires raged unchecked as the water ran out. I well remember approaching the Press the following morning, and realising the worst when I saw copies of the magenta-coloured book jacket for *Poems* strewn along the gutter.

Anne worked for some years in Faber & Faber as an editor, and as secretary to T.S. Eliot. At his suggestion they published her later poetry, until Michael Schmidt brought out her *Collected Poems* for Carcanet in 1994. Among other books she has published *A Measure of English Poetry*, and has edited the poetry and prose of Thomas Traherne.

2001   VIVIAN RIDLER

Cold in March

The cutting voice of tits in trees
    Scissors out the tunnelled spring,
While hangs for airing in the breeze
    Its leaf and catkin new linen.

Sunday cars come bagging gold
    To pollen cheapened walls in town,
Too gaudy for the withered field
    That keeps its frosty nightcap down.

I, like the icebound air
    That stutters through the chaffy stalks,
Cough and sneeze, the signs of fire
    Through house of glass wherein I walk

See unwarmed, and guess the scents
    My membrane deaf as wool debars,
A one-eyed wisher of new mints
    Of life my griffin sense obscures.

Let creature once again seem noble
    Sir, and let that be soon,
For soon we find cold and trivial,
    What we throve and took fire on.

Bunhill Fields

Under cool trees the City tombs
    Extend, and nearer lie
Stones above Blake's and Bunyan's bones
    To Vivian's working days than I.

Since he is gentle, wild and good
    As you were, peaceable Shades,
There may he go within your care
    As in my heart his love resides.

Such a care as held unharmed
    The three within the fire;
Spread wings like those that led
    Tobias in the dangerous shire.

And if I fear his death too much,
    Let me not learn more faith
By sad trial of what I dread,
    Nor grieve him by my own death.

For our faith is one which may
    Convert but not console:
We shall not, except by our own will,
    Part for ever in the gape of hell.

Kirkwall 1942

Far again, far,
And the Pentland howling psalms of separation
Lifts and falls, lifts and falls between.
But present pain
Folds like a firth round islets that contain
A sheepfold and a single habitation –
Moments in our summer of success –
Or the greater islands, colonized and built with peace.

Cold knives of light
Make every outline clear in a northern island,
The separating light, the sea's green;
Yet southern lives
Merge in the lupin fields or sleepy coves,
In crowstepped gables find a hint of Holland,
And Europe in the red religious stone:
All places in the room where we in love lie down.

At Parting

Since we through war awhile must part
Sweetheart, and learn to lose
Daily use
Of all that satisfied our heart:
Lay up those secrets and those powers
Wherewith you pleased and cherished me these two years:

Now we must draw, as plants would,
On tubers stored in a better season,
Our honey and heaven;
Only our love can store such food.
Is this to make a god of absence?
A new-born monster to steal our sustenance?

We cannot quite cast out lack and pain.
Let him remain – what he may devour
We can well spare:
He never can tap this, the true vein.
I have no words to tell you what you were,
But when you are sad, think, Heaven could give no more.

For a Child Expected

Lovers whose lifted hands are candles in winter,
Whose gentle ways like streams in the easy summer,
Lying together
For secret setting of a child, love what they do,
Thinking they make that candle immortal, those streams
                                        forever flow,
And yet do better than they know.

So the first flutter of a baby felt in the womb,
Its little signal and promise of riches to come,
Is taken in its father's name;
Its life is the body of his love, like his caress,
First delicate and strange, that daily use
Makes dearer and priceless.

Our baby was to be the living sign of our joy,
Restore to each the other's lost infancy;
To a painter's pillaging eye
Poet's coiled hearing, add the heart we might earn
By the help of love; all that our passion would yield
We put to planning our child.

The world flowed in; whatever we liked we took:
For its hair, the gold curls of the November oak
We saw on our walk;
Snowberries that make a Milky Way in the wood
For its tender hands; calm screen of the frozen flood
For our care of its childhood.

But the birth of a child is an uncontrollable glory;
Cat's cradle of hopes will hold no living baby,
Long though it lay quietly.
And when our baby stirs and struggles to be born
It compels humility: what we began
Is now its own.

For *as the sun that shines through glass*
So Jesus in His Mother was.
Therefore every human creature,
Since it shares in His nature,
In candle-gold passion or white
Sharp star should show its own way of light.
May no parental dread or dream
Darken our darling's early beam:
May she grow to her right powers
Unperturbed by passion of ours.

Bathing in the Windrush

Their lifted arms disturb the pearl
And hazel stream
And move like swanbeams through the yielding
Pool above the water's whirl
As water swirls and falls through the torn field.

Earth bears its bodies as a burden:
Arms on a bright
Surface are from their shadows parted,
Not as the stream transforms these children
But as time divides the echo from the start.

Smiling above the water's brim
The daylight creatures
Trail their moonshine limbs below;
That melt and waver as they swim
And yet are treasures more possessed than shadows.

This wonder is only submarine:
Drawn to the light
Marble is stone and moons are eyes.
These are like symbols, where half-seen
The meaning swims, and drawn to the surface, dies.

Expectans Expectavi

The candid freezing season again:
Candle and cracker, needles of fir and frost;
Carols that through the night air pass, piercing
The glassy husk of heart and heaven;
Children's faces white in the pane, bright in the tree-light.

And the waiting season again,
That begs a crust and suffers joy vicariously:
In bodily starvation now, in the spirit's exile always.
O might the hilarious reign of love begin, let in
Like carols from the cold
The lost who crowd the pane, numb outcasts into welcome.

To Mark Time

For Benedict Ridler

To mark time is not to move:
Only the unkept hours drip from the clock
Or pull at the cord coiled in its groove,
The marker moveless, and the change illusion.

The sundial shows only delightful hours,
Nor seems to move although the shadow changes.
You who watch the moment, standing still
For the peace which, always coming, never will.

Look how this child marks time within his flesh
In multiplying cells whose life is movement;
Hold him in your arms and so enmesh
The moving moment, promise and fulfilment.

So nurse the joy of which the smiles speak;
See how his lashes, like the sundial's finger
Measuring only light – the heavenly light –
Mark this time in shadows on his cheek.

Bach's B Minor Mass

'Faith discerns not the images but what the images signify: and yet we cannot discern it except through the images. We cannot by-pass the images to seize an imageless truth.'

Austin Farrer, *The Glass of Vision*

There is no word but what the poem says
Nor any image but what the music does.

Credo: does it rehearse what Christian men believe?
The beat defines it and the chords receive.
Sanctus: does it cry to the unattainable height?
Only through the lung's pressure and the bow's bite.
The infinite descent of the Incarnation
Falls in the strings toward the Desolation –
A pain once known, at once to be assuaged,
For the Resurrection is to come at the turning of the page.

Yet with the final phrase we fall from grace.
Though memory may describe the voice of stars –
Those noble and night-riding spheres
Sounding for ever in this holy gyre –
Or angels of sound that upward and downward pass
On a serpentine stair in sempiternal peace,
The wonder eludes these legends, yet the ear
Has faithful echoes in its choir.

It is not to see all heaven before one's eyes
But to become the very stuff of heaven
To live within this music. Yet it dies?
O not the music, but we die from it, as even
Its author did, who never heard it wholly played.
The ear is mortal, but the heaven it had
Is truth, no likeness, and its bliss, of God.

Piero della Francesca

The body is not fallen like the soul:
For these are godlike, being
Wholly of flesh, and in that being whole.
Founded on earth, they seem to be built not painted –
These huge girls, the mountain marble and
The valley clays were mixed for them,
The cleanness of lavender and the coolness of sand,
Also the tints of the deep sea;
And from the sea were made
The shell-like apse, and the pillars that echo each other
As waves do, in the Virgin's grey colonnade.

This gentle Jerome, with his Christ nailed
To the brown hill behind his head,
In speech with a stolid Donor, could not be
(Surely) by Manichaean doubts assailed;
In bodily peace this Solomon is wise:
Nothing is tortured, nothing ethereal here,
Nor would transcend the limits of material
Being, for in the flesh is nothing to fear
And nothing to despise.
The singing choir is winged, but who would wish
To fly, whose feet may rest on earth?
Christ with his banner, Christ in Jordan's water,
Not humbled by his human birth.

Venetian Scene

(S. Giorgio Maggiore)

Fill the piazza with blue water
And gaze across domestic seas
From church to church. The tide is tame,
The streets look firm with floating marble.
Who made the sea ride in the city?
Movement is all a floating. Ride
The idle tide that smooths the steps:
Now statues ride in the blue air,
Light floats across the white façade
And seaweed over the marble stairs.

'I who am here dissembled'

To T.S. Eliot on his sixtieth birthday

Poetry is, as you said, a *mug's game*.
    The poem, written, is lost: may earn a wage
    But cannot grow, or comfort old age.
Saints move on the unbroken beam,
But poets look with a refractory eye
On decomposing light, and need to stray.
    The work is restless, restless to refuse;
    At last even the self dissembled dies.

But where the wretched bones were laid, the tree
    Softly rustled its leaves like a child clapping,
    And a bird sang out of the juniper, such a singing
Stilled the world and earned its glory's fee
    (To break the sorcery and to find relief)
    The gold chain of love and the millstone of grief.

On a Picture by Michele da Verona

of Arion as a boy riding upon a dolphin

Here is the foreign cliff and the fabled sea,
But where is the wealthy youth we read of,
Whose music charmed the dolphins, that they bore him
Out of the reach of murderous men
To Taenarus (green-marbled Matapan)?

When he played, surely the waves he filled
With music froze, and common time was stilled
As at the intricate measure of Orpheus' song,
Past in a flash and yet a lifetime long.

But here is no frozen trance: a naked urchin
Shouting dissolves the world in waves of sound;
The cavern of the winds is in his throat,
And all comes pouring out of that primal cave
In notes that harden into hills or seas.

Out of one source, brown billows and brown land;
The gondola darts like a fish, the spiny men
Are vertebrates of sea or shore, and the castle
Caught on the cliff-top like an ark is stranded.

Astride upon a winking dolphin's neck
Arion shouts and sings, his yellow cloak
Fills with the wind;
His viol is carved with the head of a rakish cat;
He is a little noisy brat;
Also, he has the world at his command.

A Matter of Life and Death

I did not see the iris move,
I did not feel the unfurling of my love.

This was the sequence of the flower:
First the leaf from which the bud would swell,
No prison, but a cell,
A rolled rainbow;
Then the sheath that enclosed the blow
Pale and close
Giving no hint of the blaze within,
A tender skin with violet vein.
Then the first unfurling petal
As if a hand that held a jewel
Curled back a finger, let the light wink
Narrowly through the chink,
Or like the rays before the sunrise
Promising glory.

And while my back is turned, the flower has blown.
Impossible to tell
How this opulent blossom from that spick bud has grown.
The chrysalis curled tight,
The flower poised for flight –
Corolla with lolling porphyry wings
And yellow tiger markings
A chasing-place for shade and light:
Between these two, the explosion
Soundless, with no duration.
     (I did not see the iris move,
      I did not feel my love unfurl.)
The most tremendous change takes place in silence,
Unseen, however you mark the sequence,
Unheard, whatever the din of exploding stars.

Down the porphyry stair
Headlong into the air
The boy has come: he crouches there
A tender startled creature
With a fawn's ears and hair-spring poise

Alert to every danger
Aghast at every noise.
A blue blink
From under squeezed-up lids
As mauve as iris buds
Is gone as quickly as a bird's bright wink.
Gone – but as if his soul had looked an instant through the chink.
And perfect as his shell-like nails,
Close as are to the flower its petals,
My love unfolded with him.
Yet till this moment what was he to me?
Conjecture and analogy;
Conceived, and yet unknown;
Behind this narrow barrier of bone
Distant as any foreign land could be.

> *I have seen the light of day,*
> *Was it sight or taste or smell?*
> *What I have been, who can tell?*
> *What I shall be, who can say?*

He floats in life as a lily in the pool
Free and yet rooted;
And strong though seeming frail,
Like the ghost fritillary
That trails its first-appearing bud
As though too weak to raise it from the mud,
But is stronger than you dream,
And soon will lift its paper lantern
High upon an arched and sinewy stem.

His smiles are all largesse,
Need ask for no return,
Since give and take are meaningless
To one who gives by needing
And takes our love for granted
And grants a favour even by his greed.
The ballet of his twirling hands
His chirping and his loving sounds,
Perpetual expectation
Perpetual surprise –
Not a lifetime satisfies

For watching, everything he does
We wish him to do always.

> *Only in a lover's eyes*
> *Shall I be so approved again;*
> *Only the other side of pain*
> *Can truth again be all I speak,*
> *Or I again possess*
> *A saint's hilarious carelessness.*

He rows about his ocean
With its leaning cliffs and towers,
A horizontal being,
Straddled by walking people
By table-legs and chairs;
And sees the world as you can see
Upside-down in water
The wavering heights of trees
Whose roots hang from your eyes.
Then Time begins to trail
In vanishing smoke behind him,
A vertical creature now
With a pocket full of nails,
One of a gang of urchin boys
Who proves his sex by robber noise –
Roar of the sucking dove
And thunder of the wren.
Terror waits in the woods
But in the sun he is brazen
Because our love is his
No matter what he does;
His very weakness claims a share
In the larger strength of others,
And perfect in our eyes
He is only vulnerable there.

But not immortal there, alas.
We cannot keep, and see. The shapes of clouds
Which alter as we gaze
Are not more transient than these living forms
Which we so long to hold
For ever in the moment's mould.

The figures frozen in the camera's record
And carried with us from the past
Are like those objects buried with the dead –
Temporal treasures irrelevant to their need.
Yes, this is the worst:
The living truth is lost,
And is supplanted by these album smiles.

What you desire to keep, you slay:
While you watch me, I am going.
Wiser than you, I would not stay
Even if I could: my hope's in growing.
My form as a dapple of sun that flies
On the brook, is changed; my earliest word
Is the call you learnt to recognize
And now forget, of a strange bird.

Yet, as the calyx contains the life of the bud
So the bud is contained within the flower
Though past in time:
The end is not more true than the beginning,
Nor is the promise cancelled by the prime.
Not only what he was, and is, but what he might have been,
In each is rolled within.
Our life depends on that:
What other claim have we to resurrection?
For now that we can contemplate perfection
We have lost the knack of being it. What should be saved
Of these distorted lives?
All we can pray is
                    Save us from Nothingness.
Nothingness, which all men dread;
Which makes us feel an irrational pity for the dead,
And fight the anodyne
Even while we long for deliverance from pain.

So, I have read,
When a man gave his darling in grief to the grave
About her neck in a locket tied
He set this urgent word –
Not to drink Lethe, at all costs not to forget.
And this is truth to us, even yet.

For if life is eternal
All must be held, though all must be redeemed.
But what can ever restore
To these sad and short-coming lives of ours
The lovely jocund creatures that we were
And did not know we were?
What can give us at once
The being and the sense?

Why, each within
Has kept his secret for some Resurrection:
The wonder that he was
And can be, which is his
Not by merit, only by grace.
It comes to light, as love is born with a child,
Neither with help nor herald
(I did not see the iris move);
Neither by sight nor sound –
I did not feel the unfurling of my love.

Choosing a Name

My little son, I have cast you out
    To hang heels upward, wailing over a world
    With walls too wide.
My faith till now, and now my love:
    No walls too wide for that to fill, no depth
    Too great for all you hide.

I love, not knowing what I love,
    I give, though ignorant for whom
    The history and power of a name.
I conjure with it, like a novice
    Summoning unknown spirits: answering me
    You take the word, and tame it.

Even as the gift of life
    You take the famous name you did not choose
    And make it new.
You and the name exchange a power:
    Its history is changed, becoming yours,
    And yours by this: who calls this, calls you.

Strong vessel of peace, and plenty promised,
    Into whose unsounded depths I pour
    This alien power;
Frail vessel, launched with a shawl for sail,
    Whose guiding spirit keeps his needle-quivering
    Poise between trust and terror,

And stares amazed to find himself alive;
    This is the means by which you say *I am*,
    Not to be lost till all is lost,
When at the sight of God you say *I am nothing*,
    And find, forgetting name and speech at last,
    A home not mine, dear outcast.

The Surprise

This year, for Christmas star I'll choose
No spangle in the sky, but rather
An earthly one – if the frost spares it.
Turquoise berry
Centred in a magenta star,
Strange fruit of the clerodendron.

White summer blossom, sickly-scented,
Held this secret, was preparing
This surprise to outlast the leaves,
A cool blue eye to startle darkness.

A Triolet for Christmas

The bells compel us to rejoice
    And to adore all new beginning:
However cracked and harsh our voice
The bells compel us to rejoice,
And spread our wings, and rise, and praise
    The Word that spoke us into being.
The bells compel us to rejoice
    And to adore all new beginning.

Diamond Wedding

For David and Alice Pennant, and for Vivian

Worship, and faith, pledged sixty years ago,
By grace persist, and though the word *endurance*
    Commonly speaks of suffering, I today
    Choose from the root word *dur* a durable joy,
    With the hardness of a substance that will last.

How wise they were then, looking for something precious
    To symbolize a love to great age grown,
Who chose this brilliant adamantine jewel:
    'Diamond is the hardest substance known.'

Poems by

C.H. SISSON

Selected by

NORA SISSON

Charles and Nora in their garden, Langport, 1994

In the Hills

Whereas I wander here among
Stone outcrops, rocks and roots
Below me tapers the peninsula
All India going to the sea.

Below, summer is a disease
Which seas surround whose glassy blue
Nothing can cool and nothing cure
But seize my heart

The jackal wandering in the woods
For I have speech and nothing said
The jackal sniffing in the plains
The vulture and the carrion crow

O jackal, howl about my bed.
O howl around my sleeping head.

In Kent

Although there may be treacherous men
Who in the churchyard swing their mattocks
Within they sing the *Nunc Dimittis*

And villagers who find that building
A place to go to of a Sunday
May accidentally be absolved

For on a hill, upon a gibbet…
And this is Saint Augustine's county.

A Duckling

I almost prayed for its departing
The tiny bird with sodden feathers
The Christian faith forbids such pity

The duckling weaker than her sisters
Crouching in straw within the hen-coop
Recedes from the immeasurable time.

So small a life with beady eye
Comfort cannot come at and none accompany
Entering among threshed ears the darkening shades.

At the Airport

Out of blue air
You descend like light
Child, not mine but me
Your heart in my mouth

But what seems similar
Across age, sex and size
Is no such matter
My look in your eyes
Brighter than in my own
My grief beside yours
Minute
And when I seem to burn
With a like flame I am
Cold ash beside you.

Cranmer

Cranmer was parson of this parish
And said Our Father beside barns
Where my grandfather worked without praying.

From the valley came the ring of metal
And the horses clopped down the track by the stream
As my mother saw them.

The Wiltshire voices floated up to him
How should they not overcome his proud Latin
With We depart answering his *Nunc Dimittis*?

One evening he came over the hillock
To the edge of the church-yard already filled with bones
And saw in the smithy his own fire burning.

Ellick Farm

The larks flew up like jack-in-the-boxes
From my moors, and the fields were edged with foxgloves.

The farm lay neatly within the hollow
The gables climbing, the barn beside the doorway.

If I had climbed into the loft I should have found a boy
Forty years back, among the bales of hay.

He would have known certainly all that I know
Seeing it in the muck-strewn cobbles below.

(Under the dark rim of the near wood
The tears gathered as under an eyelid.)

It would have surprised him to see a tall man
Who had travelled far, pretending to be him.

But that he should have been turning verses, half dumb
After half a lifetime, would least have surprised him.

The Temple

Who are they talking to in the big temple?
If there were a reply it would be a conversation:
It is because there is none that they are fascinated.
What does not reply is the answer to prayer.

Thomas de Quincey

Thomas de Quincey lying on the hearth-rug
With a finished manuscript at his side,
His bare feet in slippers and, tied up with ribbon,
There was his mind.

Of course it was stupor that he wanted
But his mind would work.
He followed the eloquence whose end is silence
Into the dark.

On My Fifty-First Birthday

I

Hare in the head-lights dance on your hind legs
Like a poor cat struggling at a rope's end.
Everything is cruelty for innocence.
If you could mark this escape from death
In your thin mind you would have eaten what I have
And, running from form to form, you would consider
The immeasurable benignity of the destructive God.

II

A great sunlit field full of lambs.
The distant perspectives are of the patched earth
With hedges creeping about. If I were to die now
No need of angels to carry me to paradise.
O Lord my God, simplify my existence.

III

The whole hill-side is roofed with lark-song.
What dangerous declivities may I not descend?
It is dark green where the horses feed.
Blackthorn and gorse open before my eyes.

IV

The gulls come inland, alight on the brown land
And bring their sea-cries to this stillness.
It was waves and the surf running they heard before
And now the lark-song and the respiration of leaves.

For Patrick Swift

The dishes are untouched
And yet I see them all
Spread out under the moon.

Quiet, which nothing spoils,
Not even appetite,
Hung on the point of wish.

Milk-white, with ruddy fruit
Only the angry heart
Is mean enough to ask.

Ice in the silver night
With the bird voices held
In silver cups, tonight.

The Garden

Am I not fortunate in my garden?
When I awake in it the trees bow
Sensibly. There is a church tower in the distance,
There are two, underneath the maze of leaves

And at my back bells, over the stone wall
Fall tumbling on my head. Fortunate men
Love home, are not often abroad, sleep
Rather than wake and when they wake, rejoice.

Drought

The sun has risen over the parched plain
Where the water was, gold drops
Fall, thicker than hay-seeds through the light
Golden the floor on which the light pours
Golden the sky beyond the dark hills.
The Golden Age has come back, with metallic hand
To touch the drought, and spring is senile.

The Red Admiral

The wings tremble, it is the red admiral
Ecstatically against the garden wall;
September is his enjoyment, but he does not know it,
Name it, or refer to it at all.

The old light fades upon the old stones;
The day is old: how is there such light
From grey clouds? It is the autumnal equinox,
And we shall all have shrunk before daylight.

A woman, a horse and a walnut-tree: old voices
Out of recessed time, in the cracks,
It may be, where the plaster has crumbled:
But the butterfly hugs the blue lias.

The mystery is only the close of day,
Remembered love, which is also present:
Layer upon layer, old times, the fish turning
Once more in the pond, and the absent.

All could not be at once without memory
Crowding out what cannot be remembered;
Better to have none, best of all when
The evening sunlight has ended.

Its fingers lighter than spiders, the red admiral
Considers, as I do, with little movement;
With little of anything that is meant:
But let the meaning go, movement is all.

For the Queen's Jubilee

What use in following
So many queens and kings,
Elizabeth of our spring,
Elizabeth of autumn now?

What use, unless you see
Music and poetry
Standing to your honour,
As we do now?

A coronation robe
May run in holes;
The Koh-in-Noor be sold
To pay the grocer:

But there were Muses once
– Muses, what do I say?
In the language of today,
Things which affront:

The severe line the draughtsman traces
Whether anyone likes it or not;
The clearly expressed thought
Which takes the smile off people's faces:

These are the Muses, it is these
Which call for no man's protection;
These it is which will be free
Against any venal objection:

It is these, too, which can save
Your reign in memory;
Your sceptre, your sway
Still live, for poetry.

Blackdown

Here was a distant and remote youth
– I saw them on waking under the old apple-tree –
And a girl smudged by time but not remote,
Withdrawn that is from him but not from me:

Wind perhaps but not much against her dress,
Enough to show the outline of a girl.
I see them both against the blackened earth
– Burnt heather, it would be, from the smell.

Walking or standing, with the sky huge
About them on all sides except one
– It might be everywhere and they hung
Among the improbabilities of youth.

What was he saying? For it is his words
Which spring as from my lips from that image.
They are obscure now but they pierced the sky,
The future, but they have not reached me.

And yet I half suspect: 'There must be something
I could do' – or 'do well' – 'I don't know what.'
But 'well' was what I meant yet this was not
Ambition, you might rather say definition.

Yet it is she has become definite;
I never did. We twist and grow together
Like old trees with their attendant ivy
And it is I who am the parasite.

The Pleasers

All that remains to tell is how, later,
I became a top person in my way
But did not reach the top after all,
Because I had not the right sort of mind

Or because, when Fortune's smile was half-formed,
I did not keep a civil tongue for her
As certainly as the best people do,
Who otherwise would never be the best.

No matter now. No matter, really, then
Though then it seemed a matter of importance
That scurvy characters should win all
– As so it seemed, and so in part it was,

As was the case no doubt in other courts
In other times, and so it always is.
The most expensive thing is innocence
Which I half-had, yet not more than half;

For who can walk in the raging world
Without fury or fear or, worse still, hope
Which is the poison which endears us most
To fortune and betrays us most at last?

We work the world we live in, and so I
Whom other times and places would have made
A different thing – as all of us are made
By times and places which we do not choose –

Wanted the vanities I saw around me
And not the good of ordinary work
Which someone has to do and which I did
My share of, I suppose I may say.

But honour, now given another name
Though not another substance, drives us on:
Ambition can take our sleep away
And it took mine, although I knew better

And know it better, probably, than you
Unless you too have known camps and courts
Or some contemporary equivalent
Where men push for distinction as defined

By the conventions of an enterprise.
It is an unfashionable confession
– All true confession is, for anything
More or less fashionable is always right.

Yet those enemies that I remember
Were silly men enough, though clever men,
But what they had which others did not have
Was more than any poison I had drunk

Which turns to bile and sometimes to anger.
They had a self to love and loved a self
Illusory as any of my own
Yet believed in without intermission

– A picture of greatness in the mind
Which convinced them before convincing others,
Or else a cynicism which betrayed
Everything but its own skill in betrayal.

So one knew how to flash beautiful eyes
And talk like a book on any subject;
One sneaked and lied because lily-livered,
Dreading all that might keep him from success.

One dreamed of triumph and enforced his dream
On any weak enough to let him have it,
For triumph needs subservience and that
Can generally be bought with promises.

The other had no strength to spread his lie
So told enough truth to please his friends
And, falsifying records when it suited,
Made sure that no critic should come near.

And both fawned and flattered when they saw
The possibility of any benefit
– The darlings of their betters, till too late
Those betters found they too had been betrayed.

But so the world is, and to complain
Is only ignorance of what must be;
Whoever seeks salvation in it for
Himself or for his friends, should take a knife.

from *Ode for St George's Day*

Holding our tiny memory
A moment till that too goes out.
Why not? For we can never doubt
The comfort of mortality.

Yet may Time's treasure still remain
Until it quietly ebbs away
Beyond our knowledge, England's day
– I cannot help it, for the pain

Of her demise is more than all
The mind can suffer for the death
Of any creature that draws breath,
And should her time come round again

Our dust will stir, not to a drum
Or any folly men devise
But to the peace which once our eyes
Met in her fields, or else in some

Of her best children, from the first.
All this is folly too and yet
Rather than any should forget
Let this sad island be immersed

In raging storm and boiling seas.
Let no man speak for her unless
He speaks too for her gentleness
And it is her he seeks to please.

from *On the Departure*
A Sequence of Six Poems

3   Muchelney Abbey

The quiet flood
Lies between hedges and turns back the light,
Black and blue like the bruises of the time
– Sheet after sheet of record where the crime
Is lost beneath the water. Rushes write
Illegibly in mud

And willows point
Downward without weeping, or else raise
Flourishing heads topping gigantic trunks.
Uneasily the shadows of dead monks
Move past an abbey in which no-one prays.
Who will anoint

The wounds they did not,
More than we do ourselves, attempt to cure?
Grey evening behind which the sun, unseen,
Sets to the sound of church-bells, which still mean
No more than echoes: and, for sure,
Nature will rot.

O come away
To death O human race! Accept no more
This watery world in which the fox and hare
Have lost their scent, in which the livid air
Promises nothing on this wasted shore
But closing day.

Yet spring may come,
Who knows? with drought and terror, or else flowers,
For time may circle back, once more pretend
A grammar of renewal without end,
A summer with its vacuum of bright hours.

The Question

Can who be what or what be who?
The question is resolved in you,
Though not *by* you, for you will say
Your many thoughts get in the way:
You think and think and therefore are.

Before you take Descartes so far
Consider how it looks to me,
Who thinks you are because I see.
Admittedly I cannot prove
That what I see and whom I love
Are interchangeable and one.
Yet no consistent theory can
Displace the woman and the man,
So either must remain for other:
And what is one without the other?
A person? And what is a person
Except a metaphysical assertion?
I hesitate to make one so
Detached from everything I know.
If what I see and touch is true,
Then what I see and touch is you.

The Best Thing to Say

The best thing to say is nothing
And that I do not say,
But I will say it, when I lie
In silence all the day.

Address To Whom It May Concern

Sirs of the army on the march,
No dance will do; we always watch.
Sirs, we shall act while you are at
Your flattening of the policeman's hat.
To your outrageous morning shine
We shall oppose the ancient mien.
Cover your ware-announcing drums:
Study the art of being dumb.
We are instructed by our bones:
Those who will know have always known.

Berlin, 1935

Poems by

ELIZABETH SMART

Selected by

SEBASTIAN BARKER

Elizabeth Smart

For me, this is the definitive Elizabeth.

SEBASTIAN BARKER

Sebastian Barker

There's Nobody Here But Us Chickens

When the elders die
Particularly rather strict ones
Like Auden,
There you suddenly are,
The unstrict inadequate
Old but not wise
Remainder,
Now foolish top dog,
Foolishly left
In the last musical chair.

The words, the works
Were always there.
But they change, or seem to,
When their makers are gone.
No nearer now
(No farther, either)
Than Byron or Blake or Thomas Traherne or Donne.

The metamorphosis starts
The chemical change
(Eliot, Dylan Thomas, Giacometti and Braque)
Cast up, cast down,
Settled, then disinterred,
Forward and back.
Reputations, by people with nothing to do,
Are footballs kicked down the years.
But the goals are never true.

That's one thing
(A slight diversion)
What I meant to say was this:
What about poor old us?
Nudging sixty or seventy or even more
Still hoping that Daddy will pick us up from the floor
And say Tut! Tut! There There
You should try to do better
Should certainly take more care.

Raise your groggy head from this rough dilemma in
Which you find yourself, though you are only feminine
And know if it's going to go on it's got to be you
(And a friend or colleague or two):
Nobody left alive can teach you or reprimand
(Drinking or winking or lending a helping hand
Is not what I mean), it's the empty air beyond
The headmaster's empty study. In fact the entire school's
Empty of masters, *you'll* have to make the rules.
Me? I'm only a learner, one of the fools,
Let me be caretaker, let the children take over.
You can't. You're alive. There isn't any cover.
Shoddy and shy and very unfit for power
They've died and made you an elder in this cold and unjust hour.

(Sorry, Empson and Barker and good Sir John:
I know you're there, but too young and flighty to lean upon.)

So their death isn't the sorrow I thought it would be, the
                                        passion and pain,
More the bewilderment of a child left out in the rain.

A Warning

This old woman
Waddles towards love,
Becomes human,
But the Muse does not approve.

This going flesh
Is loved and is forgiven
By the generous,
But houses a demon,

Hullo, my dear, sit down,
I'll soothe your pain;
I've known what you've known,
But won't again,

Though passion is not gone,
Merely contracted
Into a last-ditch weapon,
A word not dead,

A mine unexploded,
And not safe
To have near the playground
Of innocent life.

Keep clear of this frail
Old harmless person:
Fifty year's fuel
Of aimed frustration

Could shatter the calm
And scald the soul
And love fall like napalm
Over the school.

A Bonus

That day that I finished
A small piece
For an obscure magazine
I popped it in the box

And such a starry elation
Came over me
That I got whistled at in the street
For the first time in a long time.

I was dirty and roughly dressed
And had circles under my eyes
And far far from flirtation
But so full of completion
Of a deed duly done
An act of consummation
That the freedom and force it engendered
Shone and spun
Out of my old raincoat.

It must have looked like love
Or a fabulous free holiday
To the young men sauntering
Down Berwick Street.
I still think this is most mysterious
For while I was writing it
It was gritty it felt like self-abuse
Constipation, desperately unsocial.

But done done done
Everything in the world
Flowed back
Like a huge bonus.

Trying to Write

Why am I so frightened
To say I'm me
And publicly acknowledge
My small mastery?
Waiting for sixty years
Till the people take out the horses
And draw me to the theatre
With triumphant voices?
I know this won't happen
Until it's too late
And the deed done (or not done)
So I prevaricate,
Egging them on and keeping
Roads open (just in case)
Go on! Go on and do it
In my place!
Giving love to get it
(The only way to behave).
But hated and naked
Could I stand up and say
Fuck off! or, Be my slave!
To be in a very unfeminine
Very unloving state
Is the desperate need
Of anyone trying to write.

The Muse: His & Hers

His pampered Muse
Knew no veto.
Hers lived
In a female ghetto.

When his Muse cried
He replied
Loud and clear
Yes! Yes! I'm waiting here.

Her Muse screamed
But children louder.
Then which strength
Made her prouder?

Neither. Either
Pushed and shoved
With the strength of the loved
And the unloved,

Clashed, rebuked:
All was wrong.
(Can you put opposites
Into a song?)

Kettles boiling!
Cobwebs coiling!
Doorbells ringing!
Needs haranguing!

Her Muse called
In her crowded ear.
She heard but had
Her dirty house to clear.

Guilt drove him *on*.
Guilt held her *down*.
(She hadn't a wife
To lean upon).

'The dichotomy
Was killing me,'
She said, 'till old age
Came to assuage.'

'Now! Muse, Now!
You can have your way!
(Now… what was it
I wanted to say?)'

Used, abused,
And not amused
The mind's gone blank –
Is it life you have to thank?

Stevie, the Emilys,
Mrs Woolf
By-passed the womb
And kept the Self.

But she said, 'Try
And see if it's true
(And without cheating)
My Muse can do.'

Can women do?
Can women make?
When the womb rests
Animus awake?

Pale, it must be,
Starved and thin,
Like hibernating bear,
Too weak to begin

To roar with authority
Poems in the spring
So late in the autumn
Of their suffering.

Those gaps! It's decades
Of lying low;
Earth-quaked, deep-frozen
Mind askew.

Is it too late
At sixty-eight?
O fragile flesh
Reanimate!

Eschew, true woman,
Any late profligacy
Squandered on the loving of people
And other irrelevancy,

Useful in the dark
Inarticulacy,
But drop it like poison now
If you want poetry.

Let the doorbell ring
Let the fire men
Put out the fire
Or light it up again.

Sheepish and shamefaced
At nine a.m.
Till the Muse commands
Her ritual hymn,

See lucky man
Get off his knee,
And hear now his roar
Of authority!

This test-case woman
Could also be
Just in time for
A small cacophony,

A meaningful scream
Between folded womb and grave,
A brief respite
From the enclave.

What is Art? Said Doubting Tim

It's *not* leaving your mark,
Your scratch on the bark,
No, not at all
'Mozart was here' on the ruined wall.
It soars over the park
Leaving legions of young soldiers
Where they fall.

Dido cried, like a million others.
But it isn't her tears
That sear the years,
Or pity for girls with married lovers
That light up the crying I
With the flash that's poetry:
It's the passion one word has for another.

It's shape, art, it's order, Tim,
For the amorphous pain;
And it's a hymn,
And it's something that tears you limb from limb,
Sometimes even a dithyramb;
A leap from gravity,
That feels, in the chaos of space, like sanity.

The maker makes
Something that seems to explain
Fears, delirious sunsets, pain.
What does the rainbow say?

Nothing. But a calming balm comes
From Form – a missile that lasts
At least until tomorrow
Or the next day.

Slightly Rhyming Verses For Jeff Bernard's Fiftieth Birthday

My dear Jeff,
I can't say enough
how much I admire
the way you have
conducted your entire
life, and the way you have
used your marvellous Muse.
And how right she was to
choose you. Because
she's a Rare Bird who would
have retired or died
if you hadn't known how
to amuse
her, and her you.
That's one non-bogus
marriage made
on Parnassus
and *true*.

She knew
exactly what and who
she was letting herself
in for: the real You.
Drink, betting shops and pubs
are the sort of thing that rubs
her up the right way:
she'll always stay
and make you more beautiful
and witty
every day.

This is a loose love
Ode, owed
to one of my friends
who is in my special
collection of people
who make amends
for endless excruciating

boring hours
so often lived
when foolishly pursuing
stimulation,
and none occurs.

Sterne, Benchley, Leacock,
Carroll, and Nash, and Lear
are not more dear
to me than bedrock
Bernard (3).
(Do I not pay 65p.
ungrudgingly weekly,
for a fixative laugh,
uniquely Jeff?,
who has become
a consolatory
addictive to me?)

Wilde would have smiled
and been beguiled
and bright enough to know
that *you* had a better
Muse in tow
than he.
Could he see
the angelic emanations
from gutters where we
all fall, while
trying to pee,
and rise, or try to rise,
unwisely, in majesty?

And Swift is bitter
and cross
and doesn't make us
feel better
at bearing our lot,
and, in his rage
at the odds,
misses the old adage
that recurs to me

often, in every mess:
'against stupidity
even the gods
are helpless.'
He
lifted furious fists
but had no effect
on the jibbering idjits.

Your subject is not mean,
who's up, who's in,
or jockeying for position
(what a dreary sin).
Funny but kind,
your subject is justly seen
as the inexhaustible one
of nude mankind:
Yourself, in fact, drinking,
amidst the alien corn,
and explaining the amazing joke
of being born.

Your sources –
grief and love
and the Coach & Horses
and all the things we're
thinking of
but don't admit,
because they don't fit
our grand ideas of
our own importance.
You hit the
soul on the head
when it rises
out of its lying bed,
pompous with portents
above its station,
and greedy for rewards
above its ration.

But you're never snide,
and you never hurt,
and you wouldn't want to win
on a doctored beast,
and anyhow the least
of your pleasures
resides in paltry measures.

So guard, great joker God, please guard
this great Bernard,
and let 1982
be the most brilliant year he ever knew.
Let him be known
for the prince of men he is,
a master at taking out of
himself and us the piss.

If you will do this, God,
I'll be good all year,
and try to be better-dressed,
and soberer, and keep my prose-style clear,
(for this great man
is embedded in my heart)
I'll remain, Sir, then and only then,
Yours sincerely, Elizabeth Smart.

To David Gascoyne, On his Sixty-Fifth Birthday, Some Blue Himalayan Poppies, First Found On The Roof of the World By An Intrepid Hunter, And These Inadequate Verses From His Friend Elizabeth

Count the amount of us left alive
When a young man reaches sixty-five
(I paraphrase a mutual friend
But he won't mind). It's not the end
It's the new beginning I celebrate
A true success story none can emulate
Because there's none so true.
David Gascoyne, Happy Birthday to you!

Many happy returns to him
Who kept the Muse safe under his thumb
Though trapped in troubled silences for years.
Who kept, though tortured, his integrity.
It cheers each lonely soul to know such things can be.
(It certainly does me.)

I remember I was there
When fire-bombs slashed the street
I sat on the stair
Beneath your feet
Two babies in my arms
And you read Baudelaire.

As the flames leapt
And people ran with water
I clutched my daughter
And son, and wept.
You said: 'Le désespoir a des ailes
    L'amour a pour aile nacrée
    Le désespoir
    Les sociétés peuvent changer.'
You quoted Jouve.
We did not move
Until it was all quiet
And we found we were not dead.

And I remember how you stood
Uneasily at the window
And you said
'There's something horrible in the paper'
And held out the Evening Standard
With a quiet rage
With sweet friend Margery lying smashed
On the pavement, slashed
Across the front page.

Your educative silences
(Like brackets enclosing
Enormous sympathy
Too huge to speak)
Recur like essences
To strengthen me when I am weak.

Teacher, reaffirmer
Of the good;
Repudiator
Of the stupid;
Kind ignorer
Of the mediocre
(You remain always polite
To the poor human)
Accept my gratitude.

Friend through all my inarticulate years
Consoler of my so inordinate tears
Intrepid bringer of the good news
Elegant sharer of gutters, dilemmas, blues,
One among many I raise my glass to say
October the tenth is a great day
And how lucky for us you decided to come this way.

So let's take up the blue guitar
And tell the world how wonderful you are
It's true it's true it's true
Happy birthday happy birthday happy birthday to you.

Rose Died

Unstoppable blossom
above my rotting daughter
Under the evil healing
bleeding, bleeding.

There was no way to explain
the Godly law: pain.
For your leaping in greeting,
my failure, my betrayal,

shame for my cagey ways,
protective carapace;
blame for my greeting leaping
over your nowhere place.

Spring prods, I respond
to ancient notes that birds sing;
but the smug survivor says this is *after* the suffering,
a heavenly lift, an undeserved reward.

Your irreversible innocence
thought heaven now, and eternal,
was surprised, overwhelmed
by the painful roughly presented bill,

the hateful ways of the ungenerous.
But, loving the unsuspecting flower
could love urge bitchiness
as a safe protective covering?

O forgive, forgive, forgive,
as I know you would,
that my urgent live
message to you failed.

Two sins will jostle forever, and humble me
beneath my masked heart:
it was my job to explain the world;
it was my job to get the words right.

I tried, oh I tried, I did try,
I biked through gales,
brought hugs, kisses,
but no explanation for your despair, your desperate Why.

With its smile-protected face
my survival-bent person
is hurtled on by its nasty lucky genes,
its selfish reason,

and greets the unstoppable blossom
above my rotting daughter,
but forever and ever within
is bleeding, bleeding.

Poems by

DYLAN THOMAS

Selected by

AERONWY THOMAS

Dylan, the family man, with Caitlin, Aeronwy, Colm and dog Mably

FOREWORD

All the poems selected have special associations for me. For example, 'Fern Hill' introduced me to my father's work while I was still in my twenties while other poems take me back to my roots: with family and childhood locations. In particular, the poem 'This side of the truth' written for my deceased brother Llewelyn and 'Over Sir John's Hill', a landmark I could see from my bedroom window.

Of the poems I have chosen, 'Fern Hill' has the foremost position in my mind. In my twenties, I persisted in ignoring my heritage, refusing to read my father's works in order to retain my own identity. But a chance invitation by a Welsh trade organisation to read the poem out loud at the end of proceedings which included promoting Welsh clogs and clog dancing, if memory serves, changed my life. My admiration of the poem knew no bounds, reinforced by a recognition of the places described, leading inevitably to more public readings and appearances. I was then to find the poem 'After the Funeral', about the aunt who lived at Fernhill Farm a marvellously affectionate tribute for a relative that was also mine. An even closer relative, my older brother Llewelyn, had another near perfect poem written to him I discovered, 'This side of the truth'.

On reviewing my choice, there are three dramatic poems that lend themselves to a man's voice when read out loud… not that this reservation has ever held me back reading two of them in public with gusto. They are: 'And death shall have no dominion', 'The hand that signed the paper' and 'Lament' (the one I do not read). The first one was read particularly well by Emlyn Williams in his one-man show who seemed to have little trouble with the line, "They lying long shall not die windily". (In my experience a landmine.) 'Lament' was written when my father returned from yet another of his gruelling trips to America and can be read as guilt ridden and semi autobiographical. 'The hand that signed the paper' is one of his rare political poems, with a strong metre, and sadly not often recited.

'The force that through the green fuse drives the flower' pursues the theme of man being part of Nature to which he returns at death… one much favoured by the poet. It is from this

poem I have chosen my eventual epitaph poaching the line, '…
time has ticked a heaven round the stars.' (possibly giving the
word 'time' a capital letter).

I feel the choice of the poem, 'A letter to my aunt discussing
the correct approach to modern poetry' with its slightly heavy
handed humour needs some explanation. Excelling in humorous
stories, the poet writes few "funny" poems. The poem shows him
firmly part of the '30s literary scene of Fitzrovia and Soho able to
comment on literary peers with levity. It shows his lighter side as
a sought-after bar companion of those times.

It has been a wonderful experience to choose those poems that
touch the chords of my heart not just my literary judgement and
I thank Anthony Astbury, of Greville Press, for this opportunity.
I also thank my father for giving me such a wonderful array of
goodies in the sweetshop. I hope my dad would have approved
my selection as, after all, I would have argued I am an ardent fan
not just a daughter. One thing we could always agree on, given a
shared love of sweets, that from the Laugharne sweetshop and its
tantalising row of jars the boiled sweets were our favourites.

2005   AERONWY THOMAS

And Death Shall Have No Dominion

And death shall have no dominion.
Dead men naked they shall be one
With the man in the wind and the west moon;
When their bones are picked clean and the clean bones gone,
They shall have stars at elbow and foot;
Though they go mad they shall be sane,
Though they sink through the sea they shall rise again;
Though lovers be lost love shall not;
And death shall have no dominion.

And death shall have no dominion.
Under the windings of the sea
They lying long shall not die windily;
Twisting on racks when sinews give way,
Strapped to a wheel, yet they shall not break;
Faith in their hands shall snap in two,
And the unicorn evils run them through;
Split all ends up they shan't crack;
And death shall have no dominion.

And death shall have no dominion.
No more may gulls cry at their ears
Or waves break loud on the seashores;
Where blew a flower may a flower no more
Lift its head to the blows of the rain;
Though they be mad and dead as nails,
Heads of the characters hammer through daisies;
Break in the sun till the sun breaks down,
And death shall have no dominion.

The Hand That Signed the Paper

The hand that signed the paper felled a city;
Five sovereign fingers taxed the breath,
Doubled the globe of dead and halved a country;
These five kings did a king to death.

The mighty hand leads to a sloping shoulder,
The finger joints are cramped with chalk;
A goose's quill has put an end to murder
That put an end to talk.

The hand that signed the treaty bred a fever,
And famine grew, and locusts came;
Great is the hand that holds dominion over
Man by a scribbled name.

The five kings count the dead but do not soften
The crusted wound nor stroke the brow;
A hand rules pity as a hand rules heaven;
Hands have no tears to flow.

The Force That Through
the Green Fuse Drives the Flower

The force that through the green fuse drives the flower
Drives my green age; that blasts the roots of trees
Is my destroyer.
And I am dumb to tell the crooked rose
My youth is bent by the same wintry fever.

The force that drives the water through the rocks
Drives my red blood; that dries the mouthing streams
Turns mine to wax.
And I am dumb to mouth unto my veins
How at the mountain spring the same mouth sucks.

The hand that whirls the water in the pool
Stirs the quicksand; that ropes the blowing wind
Hauls my shroud sail.
And I am dumb to tell the hanging man
How of my clay is made the hangman's lime.

The lips of time leech to the fountain head;
Love drips and gathers, but the fallen blood
Shall calm her sores.
And I am dumb to tell a weather's wind
How time has ticked a heaven round the stars.

And I am dumb to tell the lover's tomb
How at my sheet goes the same crooked worm.

After the Funeral

In memory of Ann Jones

After the funeral, mule praises, brays,
Windshake of sailshaped ears, muffle-toed tap
Tap happily of one peg in the thick
Grave's foot, blinds down the lids, the teeth in black,
The spittled eyes, the salt ponds in the sleeves,
Morning smack of the spade that wakes up sleep,
Shakes a desolate boy who slits his throat
In the dark of the coffin and sheds dry leaves,
That breaks one bone to light with a judgment clout,
After the feast of tear-stuffed time and thistles
In a room with a stuffed fox and a stale fern,
I stand, for this memorial's sake, alone
In the snivelling hours with dead, humped Ann
Whose hooded, fountain heart once fell in puddles
Round the parched worlds of Wales and drowned each sun
(Though this for her is a monstrous image blindly
Magnified out of praise; her death was a still drop;
She would not have me sinking in the holy
Flood of her heart's fame; she would lie dumb and deep
And need no druid of her broken body).

But I, Ann's bard on a raised hearth, call all
The seas to service that her wood-tongued virtue
Babble like a bellbuoy over the hymning heads,
Bow down the walls of the ferned and foxy woods
That her love sing and swing through a brown chapel,
Bless her bent spirit with four, crossing birds.
Her flesh was meek as milk, but this skyward statue
With the wild breast and blessed and giant skull
Is carved from her in a room with a wet window
In a fiercely mourning house in a crooked year.
I know her scrubbed and sour humble hands
Lie with religion in their cramp, her threadbare
Whisper in a damp word, her wits drilled hollow,
Her fist of a face died clenched on a round pain;
And sculptured Ann is seventy years of stone.
These cloud-sopped, marble hands, this monumental
Argument of the hewn voice, gesture and psalm,
Storm me forever over her grave until
The stuffed lung of the fox twitch and cry Love
And the strutting fern lay seeds on the black sill.

A Letter to My Aunt Discussing the Correct Approach to Modern Poetry

To you, my aunt, who would explore
The literary Chankley Bore,
The paths are hard, for you are not
A literary Hottentot
But just a kind and cultured dame
Who knows not Eliot (to her shame).
Fie on you, aunt, that you should see
No genius in David G.,
No elemental form and sound
In T.S.E. and Ezra Pound.
Fie on you, aunt! I'll show you how
To elevate your middle brow,
And how to scale and see the sights
From modernist Parnassian heights.

First buy a hat, no Paris model
But one the Swiss wear when they yodel,
A bowler thing with one or two
Feathers to conceal the view;
And then in sandals walk the street
(All modern painters use their feet
For painting, on their canvas strips,
Their wives or mothers minus hips).

Perhaps it would be best if you
Created something very new,
A dirty novel done in Erse
Or written backwards in Welsh verse,
Or paintings on the backs of vests,
Or Sanskrit psalms on lepers' chests.
But if this proved imposs-i-ble
Perhaps it would be just as well,
For you could then write what you please,
And modern verse is done with ease.

Do not forget that 'limpet' rhymes
With 'strumpet' in these troubled times,
And commas are the worst of crimes;
Few understand the works of Cummings,
And few James Joyce's mental slummings,
And few young Auden's coded chatter;
But then it is the few that matter.
Never be lucid, never state,
If you would be regarded great,
The simplest thought or sentiment,
(For thought, we know, is decadent);
Never omit such vital words
As belly, genitals, and –,
For these are things that play a part
(And what a part) in all good art.
Remember this: each rose is wormy,
And every lovely woman's germy;
Remember this: that love depends
On how the Gallic letter bends;
Remember, too, that life is hell
And even heaven has a smell
Of putrefying angels who

Make deadly whoopee in the blue.
These things remembered, what can stop
A poet going to the top?

A final word: before you start
The convulsions of your art,
Remove your brains, take out your heart;
Minus these curses, you can be
A genius like David G.

Take courage, aunt, and send your stuff
To Geoffrey Grigson with my luff,
And may I yet live to admire
How well your poems light the fire.

The Hunchback in the Park

The hunchback in the park
A solitary mister
Propped between trees and water
From the opening of the garden lock
That lets the trees and water enter
Until the Sunday sombre bell at dark

Eating bread from a newspaper
Drinking water from the chained cup
That the children filled with gravel
In the fountain basin where I sailed my ship
Slept at night in a dog kennel
But nobody chained him up.

Like the park birds he came early
Like the water he sat down
And Mister they called Hey mister
The truant boys from the town
Running when he had heard them clearly
On out of sound

Past lake and rockery
Laughing when he shook his paper
Hunchbacked in mockery
Through the loud zoo of the willow groves
Dodging the park keeper
With his stick that picked up leaves.

And the old dog sleeper
Alone between nurses and swans
While the boys among willows
Made the tigers jump out of their eyes
To roar on the rockery stones
And the groves were blue with sailors

Made all day until bell time
A woman figure without fault
Straight as a young elm
Straight and tall from his crooked bones
That she might stand in the night
After the locks and chains

All night in the unmade park
After the railings and shrubberies
The birds the grass the trees the lake
And the wild boys innocent as strawberries
Had followed the hunchback
To his kennel in the dark.

This Side of the Truth

For Llewelyn

This side of the truth,
You may not see, my son,
King of your blue eyes
In the blinding country of youth,
That all is undone,
Under the unminding skies,
Of innocence and guilt
Before you move to make
One gesture of the heart or head,
Is gathered and spilt
Into the winding dark
Like the dust of the dead.

Good and bad, two ways
Of moving about your death
By the grinding sea,
King of your heart in the blind days,
Blow away like breath,
Go crying through you and me
And the souls of all men
Into the innocent
Dark, and the guilty dark, and good
Death, and bad death, and then
In the last element
Fly like the stars' blood,

Like the sun's tears,
Like the moon's seed, rubbish
And fire, the flying rant
Of the sky, king of your six years.
And the wicked wish,
Down the beginning of plants
And animals and birds,
Water and light, the earth and sky,
Is cast before you move,
And all your deeds and words,
Each truth, each lie,
Die in unjudging love.

The Conversation of Prayer

The conversation of prayers about to be said
By the child going to bed and the man on the stairs
Who climbs to his dying love in her high room,
The one not caring to whom in his sleep he will move
And the other full of tears that she will be dead,

Turns in the dark on the sound they know will arise
Into the answering skies from the green ground,
From the man on the stairs and the child by his bed.
The sound about to be said in the two prayers
For the sleep in a safe land and the love who dies

Will be the same grief flying. Whom shall they calm?
Shall the child sleep unharmed or the man be crying?
The conversation of prayers about to be said
Turns on the quick and the dead, and the man on the stairs
To-night shall find no dying but alive and warm

In the fire of his care his love in the high room.
And the child not caring to whom he climbs his prayer
Shall drown in a grief as deep as his true grave,
And mark the dark eyed wave, through the eyes of sleep,
Dragging him up the stairs to one who lies dead.

In My Craft or Sullen Art

In my craft or sullen art
Exercised in the still night
When only the moon rages
And the lovers lie abed
With all their griefs in their arms,
I labour by singing light
Not for ambition or bread
Or the strut and trade of charms
On the ivory stages
But for the common wages
Of their most secret heart.

Not for the proud man apart
From the raging moon I write
On these spindrift pages
Nor for the towering dead
With their nightingales and psalms
But for the lovers, their arms
Round the griefs of the ages,
Who pay no praise or wages
Nor heed my craft or art.

Fern Hill

Now as I was young and easy under the apple boughs
About the lilting house and happy as the grass was green,
　　The night above the dingle starry,
　　　　Time let me hail and climb
Golden in the heydays of his eyes,
And honoured among wagons I was prince of the apple towns
And once below a time I lordly had the trees and leaves
　　　　Trail with daisies and barley
　　　Down the rivers of the windfall light.

And as I was green and carefree, famous among the barns
About the happy yard and singing as the farm was home,
　　In the sun that is young once only,
　　　　Time let me play and be
Golden in the mercy of his means,
And green and golden I was huntsman and herdsman, the calves
Sang to my horn, the foxes on the hills barked clear and cold,
　　　　And the sabbath rang slowly
　　　In the pebbles of the holy streams.

All the sun long it was running, it was lovely, the hay
Fields high as the house, the tunes from the chimneys, it was air
　　And playing, lovely and watery
　　　　And fire green as grass.
And nightly under the simple stars
As I rode to sleep the owls were bearing the farm away,
All the moon long I heard, blessed among stables, the nightjars
　　Flying with the ricks, and the horses
　　　　Flashing into the dark.

And then to awake, and the farm, like a wanderer white
With the dew, come back, the cock on his shoulder: it was all
　　Shining, it was Adam and maiden,
　　　　The sky gathered again
And the sun grew round that very day.
So it must have been after the birth of the simple light
In the first, spinning place, the spellbound horses walking warm
　　Out of the whinnying green stable
　　　　On to the fields of praise.

And honoured among foxes and pheasants by the gay house
Under the new made clouds and happy as the heart was long,
In the sun born over and over,
I ran my heedless ways,
My wishes raced through the house high hay
And nothing I cared, at my sky blue trades, that time allows
In all his tuneful turning so few and such morning songs
Before the children green and golden
Follow him out of grace,

Nothing I cared, in the lamb white days, that time would take me
Up to the swallow thronged loft by the shadow of my hand,
In the moon that is always rising,
Nor that riding to sleep
I should hear him fly with the high fields
And wake to the farm forever fled from the childless land.
Oh as I was young and easy in the mercy of his means,
Time held me green and dying
Though I sang in my chains like the sea.

Lament

When I was a windy boy and a bit
And the black spit of the chapel fold,
(Sighed the old ram rod, dying of women),
I tiptoed shy in the gooseberry wood,
The rude owl cried like a telltale tit,
I skipped in a blush as the big girls rolled
Ninepin down on the donkeys' common,
And on seesaw sunday nights I wooed
Whoever I would with my wicked eyes,
The whole of the moon I could love and leave
All the green leaved little weddings' wives
In the coal black bush and let them grieve.

When I was a gusty man and a half
And the black beast of the beetles' pews,
(Sighed the old ram rod, dying of bitches),
Not a boy and a bit in the wick-
Dipping moon and drunk as a new dropped calf,
I whistled all night in the twisted flues,
Midwives grew in the midnight ditches,
And the sizzling beds of the town cried, Quick! –
Whenever I dove in a breast high shoal,
Wherever I ramped in the clover quilts,
Whatsoever I did in the coal-
Black night, I left my quivering prints.

When I was a man you could call a man
And the black cross of the holy house,
(Sighed the old ram rod, dying of welcome),
Brandy and ripe in my bright, bass prime,
No springtailed tom in the red hot town
With every simmering woman his mouse
But a hillocky bull in the swelter
Of summer come in his great good time
To the sultry, biding herds, I said,
Oh, time enough when the blood creeps cold,
And I lie down but to sleep in bed,
For my sulking, skulking, coal black soul!

When I was a half of the man I was
And serve me right as the preachers warn,
(Sighed the old ram rod, dying of downfall),
No flailing calf or cat in a flame
Or hickory bull in milky grass
But a black sheep with a crumpled horn,
At last the soul from its foul mousehole
Slunk pouting out when the limp time came;
And I gave my soul a blind, slashed eye,
Gristle and rind, and a roarers' life,
And I shoved it into the coal black sky
To find a woman's soul for a wife.

Now I am a man no more no more
And a black reward for a roaring life,
(Sighed the old ram rod, dying of strangers),
Tidy and cursed in my dove cooed room
I lie down thin and hear the good bells jaw –
For, oh, my soul found a sunday wife
In the coal black sky and she bore angels!
Harpies around me out of her womb!
Chastity prays for me, piety sings,
Innocence sweetens my last black breath,
Modesty hides my thighs in her wings,
And all the deadly virtues plague my death!

Over Sir John's Hill

Over Sir John's hill,
The hawk on fire hangs still;
In a hoisted cloud, at drop of dusk, he pulls to his claws
And gallows, up the rays of his eyes the small birds of the bay
And the shrill child's play
Wars
Of the sparrows and such who swansing, dusk, in wrangling
                                              hedges.

And blithely they squawk
To fiery tyburn over the wrestle of elms until
The flashed the noosed hawk
Crashes, and slowly the fishing holy stalking heron
In the river Towy below bows his tilted headstone.

Flash, and the plumes crack,
And a black cap of jack-
Daws Sir John's just hill dons, and again the gulled birds hare
To the hawk on fire, the halter height, over Towy's fins,
In a whack of wind.
There
Where the elegiac fisherbird stabs and paddles
In the pebbly dab-filled
Shallow and sedge, and 'dilly dilly', calls the loft hawk,
'Come and be killed,'

I open the leaves of the water at a passage
Of psalms and shadows among the pincered sandcrabs prancing

And read, in a shell,
Death clear as a buoy's bell:
All praise of the hawk on fire in hawk-eyed dusk be sung,
When his viperish fuse hangs looped with flames under the brand
Wing, and blest shall
Young
Green chickens of the bay and bushes cluck, 'dilly dilly,
Come let us die.'
We grieve as the blithe birds, never again, leave shingle and elm,
The heron and I,
I young Aesop fabling to the near night by the dingle
Of eels, saint heron hymning in the shell-hung distant

Crystal harbour vale
Where the sea cobbles sail,
And wharves of water where the walls dance and the white
                                                    cranes stilt.
It is the heron and I, under judging Sir John's elmed
Hill, tell-tale the knelled
Guilt
Of the led-astray birds whom God, for their breast of whistles,
Have mercy on,
God in his whirlwind silence save, who marks the sparrows hail,
For their souls' song.
Now the heron grieves in the weeded verge. Through windows
Of dusk and water I see the tilting whispering
Heron, mirrored, go,
As the snapt feathers snow,
Fishing in the tear of the Towy. Only a hoot owl
Hollows, a grassblade blown in cupped hands, in the looted elms
And no green cocks or hens
Shout
Now on Sir John's hill. The heron, ankling the scaly
Lowlands of the waves
Makes all the music; and I who hear the tune of the slow,
Wear-willow river, grave,
Before the lunge of the night, the notes on this time-shaken
Stone for the sake of the souls of the slain birds sailing.

Poems by

EDWARD THOMAS

Selected by

MYFANWY THOMAS

Edward Thomas with Myfanwy and Tommy Dodd, Steep, 1914

FOREWORD

Making a personal choice of my father's poems has been a joy and an honour. I have begun and ended with ecstatic wishes and between these a family group and a wartime one. I have not included 'my poem' with the family's, as it was years before I could forget his drawing attention to my spectacles and straight hair, but I have chosen poems I was proud to learn were inspired by actions or words of mine.

My brother's and sister's poems were inspired when my father was taking groups of men into the Essex country to learn map-reading. All the interesting place names on the large scale wartime maps that appear in those poems were preserved many years on in the names of roads, crescents, copses, buildings, farms, schools – so they were not lost.

And I felt I must point out the lovely riddle in Bron's poem, when he promises that all the place-names, 'Roses', 'Pyrgo', 'Lapwater' and so on shall be hers without rent, if she finds a blossom on furze (gorse). And as every true countryman should know, 'When furze is out of blossom, kissing is out of fashion.'

So did she have to pay rent after all?

July 2004   MYFANWY THOMAS

To My Family

Words

Out of us all
That make rhymes,
Will you choose
Sometimes –
As the winds use
A crack in a wall
Or a drain,
Their joy or their pain
To whistle through –
Choose me,
You English words?

I know you:
You are light as dreams,
Tough as oak,
Precious as gold,
As poppies and corn,
Or an old cloak:
Sweet as our birds
To the ear,
As the burnet rose
In the heat
Of Midsummer:
Strange as the races
Of dead and unborn:
Strange and sweet
Equally,
And familiar,
To the eye,
As the dearest faces
That a man knows,
And as lost homes are:
But though older far
Than oldest yew, –
As our hills are, old, –
Worn new
Again and again;
Young as our streams
After rain:

And as dear
As the earth which you prove
That we love.

Make me content
With some sweetness
From Wales
Whose nightingales
Have no wings, –
From Wiltshire and Kent
And Herefordshire,
And the villages there, –
From the names, and the things
No less.

Let me sometimes dance
With you,
Or climb
Or stand perchance
In ecstasy,
Fixed and free
In a rhyme,
As poets do.

Merfyn

If I were to own this countryside
As far as a man in a day could ride,
And the Tyes were mine for giving or letting, –
Wingle Tye and Margaretting
Tye, – and Skreens, Gooshays, and Cockerells,
Shellow, Rochetts, Bandish, and Pickerells,
Martins, Lambkins, and Lillyputs,
Their copses, ponds, roads, and ruts,
Fields where plough-horses steam and plovers
Fling and whimper, hedges that lovers
Love, and orchards, shrubberies, walls
Where the sun untroubled by north wind falls,
And single trees where the thrush sings well

His proverbs untranslatable,
I would give them all to my son
If he would let me any one
For a song, a blackbird's song, at dawn.
He should have no more, till on my lawn
Never a one was left, because I
Had shot them to put them into a pie, –
His Essex blackbirds, every one,
And I was left old and alone.

Then unless I could pay, for rent, a song
As sweet as a blackbird's, and as long –
No more – he should have the house, not I:
Margaretting or Wingle Tye,
Or it might be Skreens, Gooshays, or Cockerells,
Shellow, Rochetts, Bandish, or Pickerells,
Martins, Lambkins, or Lillyputs,
Should be his till the cart tracks had no ruts.

Bronwen

If I should ever by chance grow rich
I'll buy Codham, Cockridden, and Childerditch,
Roses, Pyrgo, and Lapwater,
And let them all to my elder daughter.
The rent I shall ask of her will be only
Each year's first violets, white and lonely,
The first primroses and orchises –
She must find them before I do, that is.
But if she finds a blossom on furze
Without rent they shall all for ever be hers,
Codham, Cockridden, and Childerditch,
Roses, Pyrgo and Lapwater, –
I shall give them all to my elder daughter.

Helen

And you, Helen, what should I give you?
So many things I would give you
Had I an infinite great store
Offered me and I stood before
To choose. I would give you youth,
All kinds of loveliness and truth,
A clear eye as good as mine,
Lands, waters, flowers, wine,
As many children as your heart
Might wish for, a far better art
Than mine can be, all you have lost
Upon the travelling waters tossed,
Or given to me. If I could choose
Freely in that great treasure-house
Anything from any shelf,
I would give you back yourself,
And power to discriminate
What you want and want it not too late,
Many fair days free from care
And heart to enjoy both foul and fair,
And myself, too, if I could find
Where it lay hidden and it proved kind.

March the 3rd*

Here again (she said) is March the third
And twelve hours singing for the bird
'Twixt dawn and dusk, from half past six
To half past six, never unheard.

'Tis Sunday, and the church-bells end
With the birds' songs. I think they blend
Better than in the same fair days
That shall pronouce the Winter's end.

Do men mark, and none dares say,
How it may shift and long delay,
Somewhere before the first of Spring,
But never fails, this singing day?

And when it falls on Sunday, bells
Are a wild natural voice that dwells
On hillsides; but the birds' songs have
The holiness gone from the bells.

This day unpromised is more dear
Than all the named days of the year
When seasonable sweets come in,
Since now we know how lucky we are.

* The poet's birthday

Old Man

Old Man, or Lad's-love, – in the name there's nothing
To one that knows not Lad's-love, or Old Man,
The hoar-green feathery herb, almost a tree,
Growing with rosemary and lavender.
Even to one that knows it well, the names
Half decorate, half perplex, the thing it is:
At least, what that is clings not to the names
In spite of time. And yet I like the names.

The herb itself I like not, but for certain
I love it, as some day the child will love it
Who plucks a feather from the door-side bush
Whenever she goes in or out of the house.
Often she waits there, snipping the tips and shrivelling
The shreds at last on to the path, perhaps
Thinking, perhaps of nothing, till she sniffs
Her fingers and runs off. The bush is still
But half as tall as she, though it is as old;
So well she clips it. Not a word she says;
And I can only wonder how much hereafter

She will remember, with that bitter scent,
Of garden rows, and ancient damson-trees
Topping a hedge, a bent path to a door,
A low thick bush beside the door, and me
Forbidding her to pick.

                              As for myself,
Where first I met the bitter scent is lost.
I, too, often shrivel the grey shreds,
Sniff them and think and sniff again and try
Once more to think what it is I am remembering,
Always in vain. I cannot like the scent,
Yet I would rather give up others more sweet,
With no meaning, than this bitter one.

I have mislaid the key. I sniff the spray
And think of nothing; I see and I hear nothing;
Yet seem, too, to be listening, lying in wait
For what I should, yet never can, remember:
No garden appears, no path, no hoar-green bush
Of Lad's-love, or Old Man, no child beside,
Neither father nor mother, nor any playmate;
Only an avenue, dark, nameless, without end.

The Brook

Seated once by a brook, watching a child
Chiefly that paddled, I was thus beguiled.
Mellow the blackbird sang and sharp the thrush
Not far off in the oak and hazel brush,
Unseen. There was a scent like honeycomb
From mugwort dull. And down upon the dome
Of the stone the cart-horse kicks against so oft
A butterfly alighted. From aloft
He took the heat of the sun, and from below.
On the hot stone he perched contented so,
As if never a cart would pass again
That way; as if I were the last of men
And he the first of insects to have earth

And sun together and to know their worth.
I was divided between him and the gleam,
The motion, and the voices, of the stream,
The waters running frizzled over gravel,
That never vanish and for ever travel.
A grey flycatcher silent on a fence
And I sat as if we had been there since
The horseman and the horse lying beneath
The fir-tree-covered barrow on the heath,
The horseman and the horse with silver shoes,
Galloped the downs last. All that I could lose
I lost. And then the child's voice raised the dead.
'No one's been here before' was what she said
And what I felt, yet never should have found
A word for, while I gathered sight and sound.

Swedes

They have taken the gable from the roof of clay
On the long swede pile. They have let in the sun
To the white and gold and purple of curled fronds
Unsunned. It is a sight more tender-gorgeous
At the wood-corner where Winter moans and drips
Than when, in the Valley of the Tombs of Kings,
A boy crawls down into a Pharaoh's tomb
And, first of Christian men, beholds the mummy,
God and monkey, chariot and throne and vase,
Blue pottery, alabaster, and gold.

But dreamless long-dead Amen-hotep lies.
This is a dream of Winter, sweet as Spring.

Fifty Faggots

There they stand, on their ends, the fifty faggots
That once were underwood of hazel and ash
In Jenny Pinks's Copse. Now, by the hedge
Close packed, they make a thicket fancy alone
Can creep through with the mouse and wren. Next Spring
A blackbird or a robin will nest there,
Accustomed to them, thinking they will remain
Whatever is for ever to a bird:
This Spring it is too late; the swift has come.
'Twas a hot day for carrying them up:
Better they will never warm me, though they must
Light several Winters' fires. Before they are done
The war will have ended, many other things
Have ended, maybe, that I can no more
Foresee or more control than robin and wren.

from *Roads*

Now all roads lead to France
And heavy is the tread
Of the living; but the dead
Returning lightly dance:

Whatever the road bring
To me or take from me,
They keep me company
With their pattering,

Crowding the solitude
Of the loops over the downs,
Hushing the roar of towns
And their brief multitude.

The Owl

Downhill I came, hungry, and yet not starved;
Cold, yet had heat within me that was proof
Against the North wind; tired, yet so that rest
Had seemed the sweetest thing under a roof.

Then at the inn I had food, fire, and rest,
Knowing how hungry, cold, and tired was I.
All of the night was quite barred out except
An owl's cry, a most melancholy cry

Shaken out long and clear upon the hill,
No merry note, nor cause of merriment,
But one telling me plain what I escaped
And others could not, that night, as in I went.

And salted was my food, and my repose,
Salted and sobered, too, by the bird's voice
Speaking for all who lay under the stars,
Soldiers and poor, unable to rejoice.

As the team's head brass

As the team's head brass flashed out on the turn
The lovers disappeared into the wood.
I sat among the boughs of the fallen elm
That strewed an angle of the fallow, and
Watched the plough narrowing a yellow square
Of charlock. Every time the horses turned
Instead of treading me down, the ploughman leaned
Upon the handles to say or ask a word,
About the weather, next about the war.
Scraping the share he faced towards the wood,
And screwed along the furrow till the brass flashed
Once more.
           The blizzard felled the elm whose crest
I sat in, by a woodpecker's round hole,

The ploughman said. 'When will they take it away?'
'When the war's over.' So the talk began –
One minute and an interval of ten,
A minute more and the same interval.
'Have you been out?' 'No.' 'And don't want to, perhaps?'
'If I could only come back again, I should.
I could spare an arm. I shouldn't want to lose
A leg. If I should lose my head, why, so,
I should want nothing more. . . Have many gone
From here?' 'Yes.' 'Many lost?' 'Yes, a good few.
Only two teams work on the farm this year.
One of my mates is dead. The second day
In France they killed him. It was back in March,
The very night of the blizzard, too. Now if
He had stayed here we should have moved the tree.'
'And I should not have sat here. Everything
Would have been different. For it would have been
Another world.' 'Ay, and a better, though
If we could see all all might seem good.' Then
The lovers came out of the wood again:
The horses started and for the last time
I watched the clods crumble and topple over
After the ploughshare and the stumbling team.

The Cherry Trees

The cherry trees bend over and are shedding
On the old road where all that passed are dead,
Their petals, strewing the grass as for a wedding
This early May morn when there is none to wed.

A Private

This ploughman dead in battle slept out of doors
Many a frosty night, and merrily
Answered staid drinkers, good bedmen, and all bores:
'At Mrs Greenland's Hawthorn Bush,' said he,
'I slept.' None knew which bush. Above the town,
Beyond 'The Drover', a hundred spot the down
In Wiltshire. And where now at last he sleeps
More sound in France – that, too, he secret keeps.

In Memoriam (Easter 1915)

The flowers left thick at nightfall in the wood
This Eastertide call into mind the men,
Now far from home, who, with their sweethearts, should
Have gathered them and will do never again.

Lights Out

I have come to the borders of sleep,
The unfathomable deep
Forest, where all must lose
Their way, however straight
Or winding, soon or late;
They can not choose.

Many a road and track
That since the dawn's first crack
Up to the forest brink
Deceived the travellers,
Suddenly now blurs,
And in they sink.

Here love ends –
Despair, ambition ends;
All pleasure and all trouble,
Although most sweet or bitter,
Here ends, in sleep that is sweeter
Than tasks most noble.

There is not any book
Or face of dearest look
That I would not turn from now
To go into the unknown
I must enter, and leave, alone,
I know not how.

The tall forest towers:
Its cloudy foliage lowers
Ahead, shelf above shelf:
Its silence I hear and obey
That I may lose my way
And myself.

Out in the dark

Out in the dark over the snow
The fallow fawns invisible go
With the fallow doe;
And the winds blow
Fast as the stars are slow.

Stealthily the dark haunts round
And, when a lamp goes, without sound
At a swifter bound
Than the swiftest hound,
Arrives, and all else is drowned;

And I and star and wind and deer
Are in the dark together, – near,
Yet far, – and fear
Drums on my ear
In that sage company drear.

How weak and little is the light,
All the universe of sight,
Love and delight,
Before the might,
If you love it not, of night.

The Lofty Sky

Today I want the sky,
The tops of the high hills,
Above the last man's house,
His hedges, and his cows,
Where, if I will, I look
Down even on sheep and rook,
And of all things that move
See buzzards only above: –
Past all trees, past furze
And thorn, where naught deters
The desire of the eye
For sky, nothing but sky.
I sicken of the woods
And all the multitudes
Of hedge-trees. They are no more
Than weeds upon this floor
Of the river of air
Leagues deep, leagues wide, where
I am like a fish that lives
In weeds and mud and gives
What's above him no thought.
I might be a tench for aught
That I can do today
Down on the wealden clay.
Even the tench has days

When he floats up and plays
Among the lily leaves
And sees the sky, or grieves
Not if he nothing sees:
While I, I know that trees
Under that lofty sky
Are weeds, fields mud, and I
Would arise and go far
To where the lilies are.

Poems by

DAVID WRIGHT

Selected by

OONAGH SWIFT

David Wright and Oonagh Swift, *c.* 1990

A South African Album

East London, 1923

In earliest memory I hear my father.
Far off, he's calling, over the sands and sea,
A voice, invisible. I run through shallow
Lagooned and lapping water; far away

Over the water and the further shore
Where mist hangs like a cloud upon a mountain,
Horses, a herd of horses running free –
They wheel and gallop in a distant freedom,

But my hand's closed in a rough soap-yellow palm.
'Come to baas!'
As often happens in my father's country,
The first face we remember is a black one.

Monologue of a Deaf Man

Et lui comprit trop bien, n'ayant pas entendu.
Tristan Corbière

It is a good plan, and began with childhood
As my fortune discovered, only to hear
How much it is necessary to have said.
Oh silence, independent of a stopped ear,
You observe birds, flying, sing with wings instead.

Then do you console yourself? You are consoled
If you are, as all are. So easy a youth
Still unconcerned with the concern of a world
Where, masked and legible, a moment of truth
Manifests what, gagged, a tongue should have told;

Still observer of vanity and courage
And of these mirror as well; that is something
More than the sound of violin to assuage
What the human being most dies of: boredom
Which makes hedgebirds clamour in their blackthorn cage.

But did the brushless fox die of eloquence?
No, but talked himself, it seems, into a tale.
The injury, dominated, is an asset;
It is there for domination, that is all.
Else what must faith do deserted by mountains?

Talk to me then, you who have so much to say,
Spectator of the human conversation,
Reader of tongues, examiner of the eye,
And detective of clues in every action,
What could a voice, if you heard it, signify?

The tone speaks less than a twitch and a grimace.
People make to depart, do not say 'Goodbye'.
Decision, indecision, drawn on every face
As if they spoke. But what do they really say?
You are not spared, either, the banalities.

In whatever condition, whole, blind, dumb,
One-legged or leprous, the human being is,
I affirm the human condition is the same,
The heart half broken in ashes and in lies,
But sustained by the immensity of the divine.

Thus I too must praise out of a quiet ear
The great creation to which I owe I am
My grief and my love. O hear me if I cry
Among the din of birds deaf to their acclaim
Involved like them in the not unhearing air.

A Fish Out of Water

1 Highlife, Highgate

Among strangers and whisky at a contemporary saturnalia,
The music on loud and the talk kept small,
I found the failure of communication persistent
Except upon an involuntary level.

– 'Lady, forgive me, this is not my frame of reference.
Executive progressives with the right number of children,
With opinions formed by the *Statesman* and *Guardian*
– My currency of intercourse is not valid here.

'The maniacs I am at home with pursue vocations,
Few make a living and none a career.
It is a world where national insurance
Is a bigger bogey than an income-tax inspector.

'No, I am not speaking of professional bohemians,
Of those who mine for status in the stratas of culture;
I mean those who are not in the service of a competence
But of an extraneous vision, of an idea.

'You have exchanged actual for actuarial morals,
I am sure your love is free but your rent must be paid.
There is no sacrifice too dear for comfort,
If God is not there it is necessary to stay alive.

'I have to suppose I sound superior –
Yet I'd live in your world if I could. But I get bored.
And it is difficult to believe enough in the rational
Idea that all things being equal we are good.

'You attract me because I attract you. And romance
Nowadays is a mutual unveiling of genitalia;
Love a correct achievement of the sexual orgasm,
While affection hinges upon a bank balance.'

2 Poetry Reading

The reading is at the embassy. In an ante-room
Oblong and white, and hung with abstract pictures,
The nubile secretaries are offering sherry and peanuts
To poets. Homage to a contemporary culture

Is the price of the sherry. I note several names saying nothing
With notable elegance. It is, after all, their métier.
The air is heavy with amiability and prestige.
Someone tells me a lie to which I respond with another.

I am here for the drinks, and also to buttonhole Bedlam
Who has influence with Babel. This accomplished,
I am free to concentrate on getting my share of the sherry;
An anaesthetic is required if I am to face the aesthetic

Which this reception preludes. I wish I were other,
And had a purer appreciation of poetry:
A puritan bias to value art for boringness
Because it is better to suffer.

The reading begins. Seated in the auditorium
I await the return of no point, the avant-garde of Academe
Bearing dead sea fruit from a library or a museum,
And the status-poems of our cultural era.

Beside the dais two flags droop. To posit
The survival of civilization in the occidental hemisphere
I am suffering ennui in the name, I suppose, of art.
The banners are democratic. It's a cold war.

Making Verses

To Patrick and Oonagh Swift

The object of the exercise is to say
'This is what is' as clearly as I can
Until its image, mastered by a noun,
Obeys, and is the moral of the poem.
Until this happens it remains unknown.
I celebrate what is a mystery.

The image, which is of reality,
Will not be discovered, suffers no pursuit,
Will not be lured to revelation by
Sincerity of intent or hard work,
Trusts only those who only trust their luck,
Acknowledges recognition with a gay

Inclination and a wave of the hand:
And now means what it was not meant to say.
Finished, the work is praise, and will not mend
Anyone's morals or console his heart –
A function less purposive than a prayer,
It neither asks nor offers a reward.

Rhapsody of a Middle-Aged Man

These are the middle years, and I attend
Experience and the dying of the heart.
I don't feel melancholy. The idea of an end
To the world that I am cheers me up.
Only I used to feel, before, what now I know.
Enjoying more, I care for less and less,
And cherish what I do not understand –
The gaiety at the heart of mysteries.

What astonishes most is to look back and find
That there is really nothing to regret.
O my lost despairs! Where, where have you died?
Why did you go away and send me no report?
I see there is achievement in a leaf
Because it broke the bud, courage in a wall
Because it stands; a beatitude in grief
– Committed as I am to the absurd.

How can I take the universe as solemn
Seeing it's prodigal, wastes and spends,
Has no concern with thrift or responsibility
Any more than a hero with a roll of fivers
On a Saturday night taking care of his friends.
The unselective benevolence is disquieting.
What about tomorrow and the final reckoning?
He won't worry, he's the final reckoning.

As one grows older one gets caught up more
In the precipitate irresponsible gaiety.
I ought to spare time to consider the bomb
And the likelihood of no future for humanity.
But spring comes along, and trees burst into banknotes,
Or I am observing the delicate limbs of a fly
Sampling a lump of sugar on a café table.
The singing nightingales had no time for Agamemnon.

There are no consolations, none are required.
The fury and despair are the vanity.
I see the exhilaration of the numinous
Regard the tears we shed with a dry eye.
Alas, what happened? Am I no longer sensitive?
What took my tragic gown and crown away?
What leaves me standing like a fool in the huge
Gale of the universe, naked to joy?

The godhead is in the instant of being,
The Niagara of our squandered time
Sculpting its form in the movement of its falling.
No one drop more precious than the others gone
Looking for the matches, making love or a poem,
Waiting for the bus or an old age pension.
I am not called to balance such accounts or fear
Whether the waste is worth the prospect I admire.

Still one ought to end on the serious note.
I can see a number of attitudes to strike.
The trouble is they seem fundamentally comic.
And, when one thinks, it is easier to invest
In lacrimae rerum. You get a good dividend.
But how can I pull the heartstrings of a harp
I can no longer use in the ironic midday.
When he came out of hell what tune did Orpheus play,
Was it delight or frenzy that tore his bones apart?

Juxtapositions

Six decades gone and one to come,
In summer leaves I read, autumn.

July foliage, winter form:
Beech in leaf and barebones elm.

I saw a salmon leap and fail,
Fail and leap where water fell.

A wake of wild geese flying by
A river mirroring their sky.

Low river, slow river, heron
Slow also, loth to go, going.

For George Barker at Seventy

I see rain falling and the leaves
Yellowing over Eden, whose
Brown waters flood below the house
Where, thirty-five years on, I live.

So long it is since first we met,
And in another world, it seems,
Where, out of pocket, down at heels,
Night after night in Rathbone Place

The kings of Poland, and nowhere,
The out of kilter, or the good
For nothings, unfit misfits who'd
Been called to follow no career,

Would find themselves, and tell the truth.
Those great originals have gone,
They're either dead or on the wagon,
Shelved in a library, or the Tate:

But, like the Abbé, you survive.
The rain has stopped, and here's the sun
Bright gold, although it's weltering:
The skies clear, and the leaves alive.

In Memoriam David Archer

At the corner of a bar, lit by opaque windows,
Times and *New Statesman* still in their newsagent's folds, tucked
Under a withered arm shut like the wing of a bird,
Worried, inarticulate, dressed like a chief clerk,

David Archer that was, in the Wheatsheaf or Black Horse
– On Sundays at Notting Hill, the Old Swan or Windsor Castle,
A folder of plans toward some communal service
Clipped under the defeated arm as often as not.

A diffident but fanatic man; courteous;
Easily frightened; recovering courage, he'd look
Sidelong through spectacles, again like a bird, sharp and scared:
'I'm shaking like an aspirin tree. What'll you have?'

Neutral in a dark suit, holding a glass of Guinness,
That was his role and how he stood when the myths were made,
As necessary as a background and as modest,
Where they talked, struck light and took fire over his head.

Poured away and wasted like all valid sacrifice,
Libation of a subsistence. Died at Rowton House.
Impractical. Gone to immaterial reward
Along with Colquhoun and MacBryde, and Dylan Thomas.

Meetings

To David Gascoyne

Forty years ago we met
In a room in Beaumont Street.
Summer at Oxford: in St Giles,
By the Eagle and the Child
A candelabra is lit,
And chestnut petals drift.
I see you, tall and serious,
Angular, pacific, like
Some Anglo-Saxon image in
A psalter, a marginal saint.
I did not know who you were then,
But recognized the authentic,
So seldom to be met again:
What Kavanagh used to talk
About, 'the true Parnassian';
He knew, like you and Jack Yeats, that
The top of Parnassus is flat.

Other meetings, other years:
Venice in 1950, when
You stayed with Peggy Guggenheim,
But I would not meet millionaires;
Later in Paris, where you talked
As I'd not heard you talk before,
And at the dinner which you cooked,
I met Madame Picabia.
Few meetings in divided lives,
But those few were luminous
With the epiphanic commonplace:
Like your Woodbine packet seen
Inscribed 'mene, tekel, upharsin'.
Perhaps the best of all was when
Under Tennyson's Blackdown,
Together with your friend and mine
(Call him the tenant of Hearne Farm),
We paced along the sacred grove
– A ragged hedge and a few trees,

And only sacred because loved –
And watched the English evening fade
And darkness thickening the leaves,
Where no word needed to be said.

Letter to C.H. Sisson

Dear Charles,
    I think that we first met
At Henekey's in Kingley Street,
And more than twenty years ago.
You'd not find two men more unlike –
I mean the civil servant who
Was always civil (servant to
The devil, as he defined it)
And the habitué of Soho
Who'd never had a proper job,
Like nearly everyone he knew –
George Barker, Cronin, Kavanagh,
Bacon, the Roberts, Swift and Freud,
Maclaren-Ross and John Heath-Stubbs,
Gascoyne and Sydney Graham too –
There's not much left now of that crowd.
And yet it seems we understood
Each other, if I may say so,
Before we actually met:
Your verses opened on my desk
Up in that garret in New Row
The vision, spare and authentic,
Of an intellect I now know
As savage, luminous, and just.
    But let me cavil if I may:
A matter of temperament
Perhaps; but even now I find
For all that you appreciate
The underlay of the absurd
Beneath each surface, comedy
Of things as much as *lacrimae*
Rerum, I'd say your outlook is

– Although justified by logic –
One that, to what I call my mind,
Appears inordinately bleak:
Nihilistic would be the word,
But that, against all evidence,
You celebrate what is, and God.

This is supposed to be, however,
A congratulatory birthday letter,
And not an exercise in lit. crit.
I think perhaps it would be better
To turn on the nostalgia, and
Recall those evenings at the Ship
And Shovel, under Charing Cross,
And all those trains you used to miss
That ran from there to Sevenoaks;
Evenings with Higgins, Cliff, and Swift,
And Kavanagh glowering over
Scotch and bicarbonate of soda,
Those Celtic twilights of the past;
Or to recall the Dorset lanes
Haunted the less by Hardy's ghost
Than by the verse of William Barnes,
For you, most English of English;
Recall also, last but not least,
At Bemerton, the frugal church
George Herbert made a temple of:
For here I followed where you led.

Time I signed off: I hope that I
May follow you to seventy!
I see you in your evening room
High above Parrett and the moors
Stretched to the trembling of a sky
Closed over Alfred's and Arthur's
Lands, the England of your eye
Made of the living and the dead,
And on the horizon a tower.
Happy returns.

As ever,
David.

E.P. at Westminster

Old whitebearded figure outside the abbey,
Erect, creating his own solitude,
Regards, tremulously, an undistinguished crowd,
Literati of the twentieth century.
They have come to pay homage to his contemporary;
He, to a confederate poet who is dead.
The service is over. Fierce and gentle in his pride,
A lume spento, senex from America,

He can only remember, stand, and wonder.
His justice is not for us. The solitary
Old man has made his gesture. Question now
Whom did the demoded Muse most honour
When she assigned with eternal irony
An order of merit and a cage at Pisa?

Those Walks We Took

Those walks we took I shall not take
Again. The meadows sloping to
A wooded, sunken, mud-brown beck
Where, brilliant, a kingfisher flew
A flash beneath a wooden bridge,
I shall not see: but recollect,
And so preserve a living Now
In which my loss may figure like
The autumnal and failing light
That washed the fields with dying gold.

Often we walked along that beck
And crossed its rotting bridge to find
The white farmhouse below the falls
Sometimes Niagara, sometimes
A straggle like a gap-toothed comb:
And where its water dug a pool
Were Christmas geese, and water-fowl,
Making a picture for the mind
To keep – no, not for ever, but
As long as one of us had breath.

The Tomb of Virgil

From Angelo di Costanza

O you fortunate swans, who sentinel
     The windings of the lucky Mincius, say
     Whether among your nests was born (reply
If this be true) our poet, great Virgil?
May peace surround your bones, fair Siren! Tell
     Where it pleased him those hours to pass away
     Filled with calm joy; or, when he came to die,
     Whether it was in your soft lap he fell?
What better gift or favour might he have
     From Fortune, so to end as he began?
     What was more like his cradle than his grave?
The silver-throated swans, when he was born,
     Made gentle music; destined at his death
     By the cloaked Sirens to be darkly sung.

A Funeral Oration

Composed at thirty, my funeral oration: Here lies
David John Murray Wright, 6' 2", myopic blue eyes;
Hair grey (very distinguished looking, so I am told);
Shabbily dressed as a rule; susceptible to cold;
Acquainted with what are known as the normal vices;
Perpetually short of cash; useless in a crisis;
Preferring cats, hated dogs; drank (when he could) too much;
Was deaf as a tombstone; and extremely hard to touch.
Academic achievements: B.A., Oxon (2nd class);
Poetic: the publication of one volume of verse,
Which in his thirtieth year attained him no fame at all
Except among intractable poets, and a small
Lunatic fringe congregating in Soho pubs.
He could roll himself cigarettes from discarded stubs,
Assume the first position of Yoga; sail, row, swim;
And though deaf, in church appear to be joining a hymn.
Often arrested for being without a permit,

Starved on his talents as much as he dined on his wit,
Born in a dominion to which he hoped not to go back
Since predisposed to imagine white possibly black:
His life, like his times, was appalling; his conduct odd;
He hoped to write one good line; died believing in God.

NOTES ON THE POETS
AND SELECTORS

George Barker was born in Essex in 1913 and educated at the Regent Street Polytechnic. He taught English Literature at a Japanese university in 1939 and was in America from 1940 to 1943. Later he spent many years in Italy before returning to England, living in Norfolk until he died in 1991.

Elspeth Barker was born in Scotland and educated there and at Oxford. She is the mother of five children. She is a novelist, short-story writer and teacher of creative writing. Her novel *O Caledonia* won the David Higham Prize.

Thomas Blackburn was born in Cumbria in 1916. Educated at Durham University, he was Gregory Poetry Fellow at Leeds University (1956–8) and Head of the English Department at the College of St Mark and St John, Chelsea (1960–73). He wrote novels, memoirs, musicals and plays for radio, as well as poetry. He died in 1977.

Julia Blackburn, Thomas Blackburn's daughter, lives in Suffolk and Italy with her husband. A novelist and biographer, amongst her books are *The Book of Colour*, *The Emperor's Last Island* and *With Billie*.

Lawrence Durrell was born in India in 1912. He was educated at St Edmund's School, Canterbury. He spent most of his life in the Mediterranean area. He became famous for his Alexandrian Quartet novels. He also wrote travel books, including *Prospero's Cell* and *Bitter Lemons*. He died in 1990.

Françoise Kestsman Durrell first met Lawrence Durrell in 1974. She is a writer, translator and teacher and was his faithful companion for the last ten years of his life. She continues to live in the south of France.

David Gascoyne was born in 1916 in Harrow and educated at Salisbury Cathedral Choir School. He lived for many years in France, where he became friends with several French poets whose work he subsequently translated. In 1996 the French Ministry of Culture made him a Chevalier dans l'Ordre des Arts et Lettres for his services to French literature.

Apart from poetry, Enitharmon Press have published his *Selected Prose 1934–1996*, *Journal 1936–1937* and *Paris Journal 1937–1939*. He died on the Isle of Wight in 2001.

Judy Gascoyne first married a veterinary surgeon, Michael Lewis, and brought up a family on the Isle of Wight. Later, alone, she met and subsequently married David Gascoyne in 1975. She has been a lifelong teacher of French.

W.S. Graham was born in Greenock in 1918. After completing an apprenticeship in engineering, he went to study philosophy and literature at Newbattle Abbey. Starting out in a caravan in Cornwall in 1943, he dedicated his life to writing. *The Nightfisherman: Selected Letters* provides remarkable insights into his life and ideas. He died in 1986.

Nessie Dunsmuir was born in 1909, the daughter of a miner in Blantyre. She studied with W.S. Graham at Newbattle Abbey in 1938. They married in 1954 and she strongly supported his work. Her own poems were published in magazines during the 1940s and in two pamphlets from the Greville Press in 1985 and 1988. She died in 1999.

Robert Graves was born in Wimbledon in 1895. He wrote over a hundred books, among them his account of the First World War, *Goodbye to All That*, *I Claudius* and *The White Goddess*. He died in 1985 in Deià, the Majorcan village he had made his home since 1929.

Beryl Graves was born in London in 1915. She was Robert Graves's second wife and lived with him and their four children in Majorca. After his death, she worked on the definitive three-volume *Complete Poems of Robert Graves*, published by Carcanet. She died in Deià in October 2003.

Harold Pinter was born in the East End of London in 1930 and educated at Hackney Downs Grammar School. He became an actor and subsequently began to write plays. Amongst his many plays are *The Caretaker*, *The Birthday Party* and *The Homecoming*. He has also written several film scripts. In 1995 he won the David Cohen British Literature Prize for a lifetime's achievement in literature and was made a Companion of Honour in 2002.

Antonia Fraser has written eight historical biographies, most recently *Marie Antoinette: The Journey*. She has edited *Scottish Love Poems*, an anthology for Canongate Publishing, and *Love Letters* for Orion. She also edits the 'Kings and Queens of England' series.

Anne Ridler was born in 1912, the daughter of a Rugby School house-master. She was educated at Downe House School, in Italy and King's College, London. She worked on the editorial staff at Faber and Faber, for a time as assistant to T.S. Eliot, and later as a freelance reader. She was the mother of four children. Apart from poetry she wrote verse plays and translated the librettos of several operas. She was appointed OBE in 2000 and died in 2001.

Vivian Ridler, Anne Ridler's husband, was born in 1913 and educated at Bristol Grammar School. He was Printer to the University of Oxford from 1958 to 1978. He was made CBE in 1971 and Emeritus Fellow of St Edmund Hall in 1978. He continues to print through his Perpetua Press, Oxford.

C.H. Sisson was born in Bristol in 1914 and educated at the University there and then in Germany and France. He entered the civil service, rising to Under-Secretary in the Ministry of Labour, before taking early retirement in 1974. A novelist, essayist and translator as well as a poet, he was made a Companion of Honour for services to literature in 1993. He died in 2003.

Nora Sisson was born in Sheffield in 1914. In 1927 her family moved to Bristol, where she first met C.H. Sisson at Fairfields Secondary School. She read history at Somerville College, Oxford and taught history in London for some years. She married C.H. Sisson in 1937 and they had two daughters. She died in 2003.

Elizabeth Smart was born in Canada in 1913. She worked during the Second World War for the British Embassy in Washington D.C. before being transferred to the Ministry of Information in London in 1943. She was the mother of four children by George Barker, and supported herself and family with journalism and advertising work. Apart from poetry, she wrote the autobiographical *By Grand Central Station, I Sat Down and Wept* and the novel *The Assumption of the Rogues and Rascals*. She died in 1986.

Sebastian Barker is the son of Elizabeth Smart and George Barker. His books of poetry include *Guarding the Border: Selected Poems* and *The Hand in the Well*. He also has written a documentary novel, *Who is Eddie Linden*. He was elected a fellow of the Royal Society of Literature in 1997 and in 2002 became the editor of *The London Magazine*.

Dylan Thomas was born in Swansea in 1914 and educated at the Grammar School there. He rapidly established himself as one of the finest poets of his generation. Throughout his life he wrote short stories, his most famous collection being *Portrait of the Artist as a Young Dog.* He also wrote film scripts, poems and talks, lectured in America and wrote the radio play *Under Milk Wood.* He died in 1953.

Aeronwy Thomas, Dylan Thomas's daughter, was born in 1943. She is now married to a Welshman and has two children. She has talked about her father and lectured on his work in Britain, Europe and America. She has published a number of poems and reminiscences of her father, including *Later Than Laugharne* and *Poems and Memories.*

Edward Thomas was born in 1878. He was educated at St Paul's School and Lincoln College, Oxford. Apart from poetry, he wrote critical biographies of various writers and nature books. He served in the Artists' Rifles in the First World War and fell at the battle of Arras in 1917.

Myfanwy Thomas, Edward Thomas's youngest daughter, was born in 1910. Her account of her childhood was included in Helen Thomas's memoir *Under Storm's Wing.* After the Second World War she trained to be a teacher and taught for twenty-one years at two schools in Lambourn, Berkshire. She died in 2005.

David Wright was born in South Africa in 1920 and came to England at the age of fourteen to attend the Northampton School for the Deaf. He graduated from Oriel College, Oxford, in 1942. From 1959 to 1962 he edited, together with Patrick Swift, the magazine *X.* He selected several definitive anthologies including *The Faber Book of Twentieth Century Verse* (with his friend John Heath-Stubbs) and a memoir *Deafness: A Personal Account.* He died in 1994.

Oonagh Swift, born in Dublin 1929, was educated at Mount Anvill Convent and later in Brussels, where she met her first husband, Prince Alexis Guedroitz, by whom she had a daughter, Ania, in 1959. The marriage ended in 1962. She married Patrick Swift the painter and co-editor, with David Wright, of *X* magazine, with whom she had three daughters. Together they revived Portuguese majolica ware in the Algarve. After Patrick Swift's death she married David Wright in 1988.

ACKNOWLEDGEMENTS

GEORGE BARKER: 'Allegory of the Adolescent and the Adult', 'To My Mother', 'Summer Song I', 'Turn on your side and bear the day to me', 'Galway Bay', 'Roman Poem III', 'At Thurgarton Church', 'Morning in Norfolk', excerpts from 'Villa Stellar' I, LVIII © The Estate of George Barker, from *Selected Poems* (Faber & Faber, 1995), reprinted by permission of the publisher; 'A Version of Animula Vagula Blandula' © The Estate of George Barker, from *Street Ballads* (Faber & Faber, 1992), reprinted by permission of the publisher; 'Battersea Park', 'On a Friend's Escape from Drowning off the Norfolk Coast' © The Estate of George Barker, from *Collected Poems 1930–1955* (Faber & Faber, 1957), reprinted by permission of the publisher; selection, photograph and foreword © Elspeth Barker, 2004, 2005.

THOMAS BLACKBURN: poems from *Selected Poems* (Carcanet Press, 2001) © The Estate of Thomas Blackburn, reprinted by permission of the publisher; selection and photograph © Julia Blackburn 1999, 2005.

LAWRENCE DURRELL: 'Highwayman', excerpt from 'Cities, Plains and People', 'Song for Zarathustra', 'Sarajevo', 'The Octagon Room', 'Eleusis', 'The Ikons', 'The Outer Limits', from *Collected Poems* (Faber & Faber, 1960) reproduced with permission of Curtis Brown Ltd, London on behalf of The Estate of Lawrence Durrell and by permission of the publisher, copyright © The Estate of Lawrence Durrell 1931, 1946, 1948, 1951, 1956, 1961, 1966, 1968; 'Feria: Nîmes', 'Le cercle refermé' from *Caesar's Vast Ghost: Aspects of Provence* (Faber & Faber, 1990), reproduced with permission of Curtis Brown Ltd, London on behalf of The Estate of Lawrence Durrell and by permission of the publisher, copyright © the Estate of Lawrence Durrell 1990; selection and foreword © Françoise Kestsman Durrell, 2005; photograph © Francis Giacobetti, 1987, 2005.

DAVID GASCOYNE: poems from *Selected Poems* (Enitharmon Press, 1994) © The Estate of David Gascoyne 2005, reprinted by permission of the publisher; selection, foreword and photograph © Judy Gascoyne 2001, 2005.

W.S. GRAHAM: poems from *Collected Poems* (Faber & Faber 1979) © The Estate of W.S. Graham, 1998, 2005; photograph © Michael Snow, 1998, 2005.

Trustees for the copyrights of Dylan Thomas. Reprinted by permission of New Directions Publishing Corp.; 'In My Craft or Sullen Art', from *The Poems of Dylan Thomas*, copyright © 1946 by New Directions Publishing Corp. Reprinted by permission of New Directions Publishing Corp.; 'A Letter to My Aunt Discussing the Correct Approach to Modern Poetry', 'Lament', 'Over Sir John's Hill', 'This Side of the Truth', from *The Poems of Dylan Thomas*, copyright © 1952 by Dylan Thomas. Reprinted by permission of New Directions Publishing Corp. 'The Conversation of Prayer', from *The Poems of Dylan Thomas*, copyright © 1967 by the Trustees for The Copyrights of Dylan Thomas. Reprinted by permission of New Directions Publishing Corp. Selection, foreword and photograph © Aeronwy Thomas 2005.

EDWARD THOMAS: selection, foreword and photograph © The Estate of Myfanwy Thomas 2004, 2005.

DAVID WRIGHT: poems from *To the Gods the Shades* (Carcanet Press, 1976) and *Selected Poems* (Carcanet Press, 1988) © The Estate of David Wright, reprinted by permission of the publisher; selection and photograph © Oonagh Swift 2003, 2005.

Every effort has been made to trace the copyright holders of the poems published in this book. The editor and publishers apologise if any material has been included without the appropriate acknowledgement, and will be glad to correct any oversights in future editions.